*Endorsements*

Throughout history God has place unique men and women to bridge the gap between the institutional church and marketplace. Sir George Williams founder of the YMAC and D. L. Moody were out of the box thinkers that changed their culture. Rex Wolins is of the same mold, he is able to see beyond the confined of church and business world. By virtue of his sensitivity to scripture & practical business wisdom, he weaves a unique tapestry called Everyday Optimum Leadership. This book is a fresh look at accessible leadership.

**Javier F. Rodriguez**

**President / RISCO Insurance Services, Inc**

For the thirty-plus years I have known and worked with Rex, he has been one of the most innovative, entrepreneurial and effective persons I have ever met. He has produced in *Everyday Optimum Leadership* a solid powerful tool for improving leadership. More than that, for aiming leadership in directions that produce fruitful organizations, churches, and people's lives long term. Responsible, value-centered, forward leadership—Rex has done it again!

**Dr. Jim Price**

**Senior Pastor**

**Diamond Canyon Christian Church**

The rapidly changing world presents new challenges and opportunities for leadership. The ideas and attitudes that once drove businesses need to be updated. Leadership is no longer an option. But for most it remains an enigma. This book offers important insights in acquiring these leadership skills. It's not just a book. It's an action plan and a road map that leads to success. Every home and offices need to have a copy of this book.

**Dr. Ola B. Madsen**

**President of E.O. International Inc.**

# EVERYDAY
# OPTIMUM LEADERSHIP

*Practicing Servant Leadership - Other Centered Focused*

## R. G. WOLINS

WestBow
PRESS
A DIVISION OF THOMAS NELSON

WestBow Press books may be ordered through booksellers or by contacting:

WestBow Press
A Division of Thomas Nelson
1663 Liberty Drive
Bloomington, IN 47403
www.westbowpress.com
1-(866) 928-1240

Because of the dynamic nature of the Internet, any web addresses or links contained in this book may have changed since publication and may no longer be valid. The views expressed in this work are solely those of the author and do not necessarily reflect the views of the publisher, and the publisher hereby disclaims any responsibility for them.

Any people depicted in stock imagery provided by Thinkstock are models, and such images are being used for illustrative purposes only.

Certain stock imagery © Thinkstock.

ISBN: 978-1-4497-3626-2 (sc)
ISBN: 978-1-4497-3627-9 (e)

Library of Congress Control Number: 2011963666

Printed in the United States of America

WestBow Press rev. date: 1/27/2012

# Dedication

First I dedicate this work to my Lord and Savior Jesus Christ,
for the discipline of Servant Leadership
Is simply following what He has told us in His word.
Secondly to my beautiful wife Shi Mei who has been at my side for
over 40 years.
She has been my light in dark times, the voice of reason
when I would go in the wrong direction.
I was blessed by God the day I first met her for
She is truly a Proverbs 31:10-31 wife.

# *Epigraph*

Leaders we admire do not place themselves at the center; they place others there. They do not seek the attention of people; they give it to others. They do not focus on satisfying their own aims and desires; they look for ways to respond to the needs and interests of their constituents. They are not self-centered; they concentrate on the constituent . . . Leaders serve a purpose and the people who have made it possible for them to lead . . . . In serving a purpose, leaders strengthen credibility by demonstrating that they are not in it for themselves; instead, they have the interests of the institution, department, or team and its constituents at heart. Being a servant may not be what many leaders had in mind when they choose to take responsibility for the vision and direction of their organization or team, but serving others is the most glorious and rewarding of all leadership tasks."

**—by James Kouzes and Barry Posner in Credibility: How Leaders Gain and Lose It, Why People Demand It.**

# Table of Contents

Chapter I:    Core values / attributes or inward traits of the
              Everyday Optimum Leader ........................................... 1

*Honesty* ...................................................................... *3*
*Forward-looking* ............................................................. *5*
*Competency* .................................................................. *7*
*Intelligence* ................................................................ *8*
*Fair-minded* ................................................................ *10*
*Courageous* ................................................................. *10*
*Imaginative* ................................................................ *10*

Chapter II:   Practice makes <u>perfect</u> = Mature .............................. 17

*Empowered Leadership* ...................................................... *19*
*Ethical Leadership* ........................................................ *21*
*Enabling Leadership* ....................................................... *24*
*Effective Leadership* ...................................................... *26*
*Efficient Leadership* ...................................................... *28*

Chapter III:  Making an Optimum Decision ....................................... 33

*Draw upon Christian faith resources* ....................................... *38*
*Follow a basic decision process* ........................................... *41*
*Identify a basic decision process* ......................................... *44*
*Involve the right people* .................................................. *44*
*State the guiding objectives and priorities* ............................... *48*
*Gather decision-making information* ........................................ *48*
*Clearly state and evaluate the options* .................................... *52*
*Make and implement the decision* ........................................... *52*
*Assess the effectiveness of the decision and process* ...................... *56*
*Identify and avoid common mistakes* ........................................ *56*

Chapter IV:   A decision that can bring down a leader ..................... 61

*"Beware your sins will find you out"* ............................................. *61*

Chapter V:   Walking on the edge of a wrong decision .................. 81

*Moral Failure and the leader* ............................................................ *90*
*What can we learn from fallen Christian leadership?* ............................ *92*
*Rescuing the fallen leader, in the church and the marketplace* .................... *97*

Chapter VI:   Optimum Leadership Instruments HANDS ON ....... 103

*Multifactor leadership questionnaire* ............................................... *105*
*Style questionnaire* ...................................................................... *108*
*Putting yourself in the picture* ...................................................... *110*
*People skills* ............................................................................... *115*
*Win people to your way of thinking* ................................................ *117*
*Be an everyday optimum leader* ..................................................... *118*
*Coping style questionnaire* ........................................................... *120*

Chapter VII:  Optimum Attitude, Expectation, Power & Success ..... 123

*Anatomy of an everyday optimum leader* .......................................... *125*
*Attitude check-up – Dealing with pride* ............................................ *127*
*Expectation theory* ...................................................................... *135*
*The power of forgiveness* ............................................................... *136*
*Success* ..................................................................................... *143*

Chapter VIII: Optimum Leadership Keys to: ............................... 153

*Making Change* ......................................................................... *155*
*Setting Goals* ............................................................................. *162*
*Communication* ......................................................................... *170*
*Dealing with stress* ..................................................................... *174*

Chapter IX:  Knowing discouragement Knowing failure
            And 11 tips to move beyond ..................................... 185

*Ways to fail as a leader* ............................................ *187*
*Tip 1 Optimum leadership* ....................................... *195*
*Tip 2 Staying young your whole life* ............................ *196*
*Tip 3 The unexamined life becomes a liability* .................... *198*
*Tip 4 What makes an optimum leader?* .......................... *199*
*Tip 5 Things a leader creates* ..................................... *200*
*Tip 6 Three ways to kill creative leadership* ..................... *203*
*Tip 7 Three abilities to look for* ................................. *203*
*Tip 8 Three questions to ask* ..................................... *204*
*Tip 9 The benefits of good leadership are* ......................... *205*
*Tip 10 The cost of bad leadership* ................................ *206*
*Tip 11 Empowerment...the effect of leadership* .................. *206*

Chapter X:   Final laws of Optimum Leadership ........................... 209

*Secrets of happiness* ............................................... *212*
*What people want from their leaders* ............................. *217*
*Suggestions for a brighter future* ................................. *217*
*Life-changing declarations* ........................................ *218*
*Positive self-affirmations* .......................................... *220*
*Things to remember* ............................................... *220*
*How to get out of the rut and stay out* ........................... *221*
*Declaration of self-esteem* ......................................... *222*

# Forward

The audience for this work is a broad one, the man or woman that desires to move to a new level in their pursuit to be a better leader. They may be a Christian or may not. In general this book is geared toward a fresh look at accessible leadership. As you read though the book, hopefully you will take the "Leadership Instruments," these will help give you a true idea of the kind of leader you are and the kind of leader you can be.

Allow the Lord to speak to your heart about Servant Leadership and becoming what this work calls "Other Centered Focused." The take-ways from this book are not that profound or lofty but remain down to earth and practical for the person who wants to follow the greatest servant leader in history, Jesus Christ.

In today's world the person working in a business, public office or even in a church finds themselves in a culture devoid of even the basic elements talked about in this book. As stated at the beginning of the book, it was not Rex's intention to write another boring book on leadership, but to present many of what he calls HANDS ON and SNAPSHOOT bits to move the reader from one point to the next not necessarily connecting the two together but having each chapter and sometimes each page develop a brand new idea, tidbit or nugget to think about.

In reading this work it delivers just what it promises, and that is to help move the reader from where they are into an optimum future.

Most books and seminars on leadership assume that the essence of the subject is already well known and the basis of it generally agreed upon by the readers or seminar participants. Thus they tend to deal largely with the refinements of the craft, or the ways of improving leadership performance by the use of organization theory and management technology. It is no wonder then if leaders get the message that to lead effectively one must be a good administrator and learn to use the manager's techniques, or the managers using the tools they are familiar with, think that in so doing they are leading. This work takes on a fresh new different approach.

What then is the essence of the essential heart of this thing we call leadership? In other words, what are the features that distinguish leadership from other people in the organization, and the leadership role from other roles or functions? This work not only answers these questions but brings the reader along a journey leading them to their optimum potential, all this based on what God has to say about being an Everyday Optimum Leader.

Enjoy your journey . . .

**United States Congressman**
**Gary Miller 42nd Congressional District**
**California**

# Preface

What is Servant leadership-both its biblical and contemporary components? How does it relate to patterns and practices in your life, the marketplace or in a church?

This working definition is a guideline for me, and I share it with you:

*Practicing servant leadership in my life, the marketplace or in a church is self-giving service with others after the pattern of Christ in order to achieve extraordinary commitment and contributions toward mutually shared goals.*

*"Brothers, I do not consider myself yet to have taken hold of it. But one thing I do: Forgetting what is behind and straining toward what is ahead, I press on toward the goal to win the prize for which God has called me heavenward in Christ Jesus."—Phil. 3:13-14 (NKJV)*

## A Servant Leadership Pattern

Visuals, definitions, concepts, the sage instruction of a pioneer like Allen Greenleaf, even Holy Scripture—all of these fall short of the mark if you and I do not get them down into "Practicing Servant Leadership" consistently. It is a way of living, serving, and leading. In a nutshell one could call it, "Other Centered Focus." Let's work through this together.

Years ago I started with the oft-quoted maxim adapted from Warren Bennis:

*"Efficiency [management] is doing things right"*
*"Effectiveness [leadership] is doing the right things."*

Placing high value on these elements, the Servant Leadership graphic on these pages intends to portray the practice of Servant Leadership or Other Centered Focus as open windows of opportunity—of light and fresh air. The largest window, encompassing all else, is **empowered leadership**; the smallest window, supporting all else, **is efficiency**. **But all of it starts on the inside and works its way outward in your life, the marketplace or in a church. Enabling a person to become an Everyday Optimum Leader.**

# It all starts deep inside of . . .
## YOU

Everyday Optimum Leadership is made up of the inward elements of the leader, the very fiber that makes them what and who they are. It does not look only on the external elements such as how one speaks, looks, or their charisma. It focuses on what goes on under the hood, what elements are needed in the heart of the true leader? Elements like attitude, character, etc. Everyday Optimum Leadership takes the elements and holds them under a microscope and examines them, each one and looks at their core power.

Let us look at some insight regarding the inner person. There was a man who lived thousands of years ago, his name was Solomon. He was arguably the wisest and richest man of his time. Here are some of the thought he had about the inner leader.

*"Dear friend, take my advice; it will add years to your life. I'm writing out clear directions to Wisdoms Way, I'm drawing a map to a Righteous Road." (The Message)*

*"I don't want you ending up in blind alleys, or wasting time making wrong turns. Hold tight to good advice; don't relax your grip. Guard it well—your life is at stake! Don't take the Wicked Bypass; don't so much as set foot on that road. Stay clear of it; give it a wide berth. Make a detour and be on your way". (The Message)*

*"Dear friend, guard clear Thinking and Common Sense with your life; don't for a minute lose sight of them. They'll keep you alive and well, they'll keep you fit and attractive." (The Message)*

"Don't walk around with a chip on your shoulder, always spoiling for a fight. Don't try to be like those who shoulder their way through life. Why be a bully?" (The Message)

"Why not?" you say. Because it will come to no end. It's the straightforward who get respect." (The Message)

"Wise living gets rewarded with honor; stupid living gets the booby prize." (The Message)

"Evil people are restless unless they're making trouble; they can't get a good night's sleep unless they've made life miserable for somebody. Perversity is their food and drink, violence their drug of choice." (The Message)

"The ways of _right-living_ people glow with light; the longer they live, the brighter they shine. But the road of wrongdoing gets darker and darker—travelers can't see a thing; they fall flat on their faces."

(The Message)

"Dear friend, listen well to my words; tune your ears to my voice.

Keep my message in plain view at all times. Concentrate! Learn it by heart! Those who discover these words live, really live; body and soul, they're bursting with health." (The Message)

—Solomon

# Introduction

## At the heart of Servant Leadership / Other centered focused

It is my desire that in writing this I would capture the heart and soul of what it means to be a servant leader or give direction to the person who is on the journey of becoming "Other centered focused." I did not want to write "just one more boring book rehashing the concept of servant leadership." I wanted to bring a fresh new, what I would call "hands on" approach. Part of this you will find when you go through the "Leadership Instruments" and also pick up on what I call "one line bite size bits to remember." As you read through the book you will see just what I am talking about.

The phrase "servant leadership" may not be familiar to a number of individuals or corporations, or for that matter to some even in the church. But it is a belief system that is already widely embraced by some of the most successful organizations and churches in the world. Its essence is a focus on individuals and a decentralized organizational structure. It also emphasizes other core values that encourage innovation and the development of leaders that must first focus on serving all stakeholders in an organization, a church or at home.

## Servant Leadership According to its Founder

The term servant leadership is attributed to an essay written by Robert Greenleaf (1904-1990) in 1970. Greenleaf's essay was entitled *The Servant as Leader* and stemmed from concerns over the merits of a centralized organizational structure as a management style to successfully run companies. This belief was undoubtedly formed in part while working at AT&T and evolved once he founded the Greenleaf Center for Servant Leadership in 1964.

First, it is important to present the concept of servant leadership from Greenleaf's perspective. He was suspicious of those focused on leading first, "perhaps because of the need to assuage an unusual power drive or to acquire material possessions," he said in his essay. Instead, he recommended making serving a priority, with the intent of "making sure that other people's highest priority needs are being served."

His focus was from an individual perspective. As he put it, "caring for persons, the more able and the less able serving each other, is the rock upon which a good society is built." He believed that this responsibility had shifted over time to institutions, which were "often large, complex, powerful, impersonal; not always competent; sometimes corrupt."

**Servant Leadership Further Defined for the marketplace**

Boiling servant leadership down to its basic terms and how it can be used to improve business performance, in essence it can represent a decentralized structure that focuses on employee empowerment and encourages innovation. This mean having upper management share key decision making powers with employees that work directly with customers that are arguably better aware of what is needed to serve clients and remain competitive because of their knowledge of what is occurring on the "front lines" of the business.

Perhaps most importantly, servant leadership is focused on serving all stakeholders in the corporation. This includes employees, customers and the community in general. It is seen as an evolution of a traditional corporate measure that emphasizes growing stakeholder returns over time. A criticism of this measure is that it can be at the expense of the other stakeholders, especially if profit is the only driver of corporate success and leads to the trampling of other stakeholders that are vital to long-term survival of an organization.

## The Primary Characteristic

For firms to remain competitive, listening is crucial. Employees must stay connected to customers and industry developments and they need to listen and remain receptive to clients. This is because those external parties frequently have significant insight into product successes and changes that could grow into challenges or ruin a firm if not addressed. Awareness and paying attention to important issues are also seen as paramount. Additionally, persuasion is suggested through consensus building and stands in direct contrast to tactics that are considered more command and control. Coercive tactics that are pushed through from more centralized organizations can be especially destructive.

From an employee development perspective, empathy means takes the point of view that customers and colleagues have good intentions. It emphasizes open-mindedness in hearing decisions. Healing might seem too soft for many corporate cultures, but at its core it emphasizes the development of individuals from both personal and professional perspectives. For instance, encouraging learning, development and constructive feedback along with the completion of job tasks is the focus of this characteristic. Foresight is similar to awareness but stresses the ability to use past lessons for success going forward. A commitment to the growth of people is also warranted, as is an emphasis on developing talent.

## Servant Leadership Defined for the church and in the home

Greenleaf brought the concept of a servant leader from scripture and applied it in the marketplace. The pathway or crossover use in the business world is a natural one and as you have just read a most effective one. Now we look at it in its first environment and that is in the church.

Servant Leadership is exercising real, Godly leadership, as Christ did when He used a towel, and influencing, equipping, and empowering people to accomplish God's purpose and plan. It is serving others unselfishly while influencing and empowering them to grow in a Christ-directed, purposeful direction. This was an uncommon trait in Jesus' time, just as it is in ours; do not let it be uncommon for you! Being a leader in the church, or in the home for a husband, is never a force of personality; it is earning that respect because you love and care (1 Kings 3:9; Luke 22:25-28; Matthew 25:21; Mark 9:33-37; John 5:19; Philippians 1:1; 1 Timothy 3:1-5; 2 Timothy 2:24; Hebrews 13:17)

**Ask yourself or Group:**

1. Are these elements working in you and in your church? If not, why not?
2. What would your business or church look like if these precepts were functioning?
3. What can you do to instill Servant Leadership in yourself and your church, your home, your life in general?

**Hint: it starts with modeling them! And, don't forget, *lots of prayer*.**

Servant Leaders give priority to others and value their opinions. They do not compare or criticize others.

They are people who have the attitudes that Jesus had!

They are people who have been transformed by Christ, with faith as the core of their being, and fuelled by Christ, not self!

They are people who place the needs of others first!

They are people who have eternal values and God's timing in mind!

They are people who place integrity ahead of ambition! (1 Tim. 3:2a & 7a)

They are people who see glorifying Christ and serving Him as the measure of success!

Servant Leaders of Jesus Christ and His church have His "basin and towel" attitude (John 13:1-17; 1 Corinthians 9:26, 27)!

Servant Leaders do not neglect their families!

Christian leaders and followers must not allow personal agendas or power issues to get in the way of God's Word or of reaching the goal of the church (if the goal is biblical).

Servant Leaders can and should expect that Satan will not be happy with them, and must be aware of his various ways of distraction and confusion, especially when success comes which infringes on his ground. The church and your home are Satan's ground all too often!!

Servant Leaders are never prideful and do not take themselves too seriously! They will never have inflated feelings about their importance or thrive on attention and admiration!

**If you are in leadership, then be a good leader!**

Be a servant with your leadership. Our attitude and behaviours will be closely watched and mimicked! We are the ones who will either encourage others to seek and know Him more, or distract them away from the church and our Lord. We must be growing in the faith with conviction and fortitude so we will have good motives. Good motives are essential to good leadership; otherwise, all you have are power plays, strife, and dysfunction! Churches that have problems, for the most part (in my experience), are mainly because the leadership has forgotten who Christ is in their personal lives, and they do not practice His precepts. They are not willing to be good followers and therefore end up leading the people with personal agendas and trends. Christ is left out of the loop (1 Kings 3:9; Luke 22:25-28; Matthew 25:21; Mark 9:33-37; John 5:19; Philippians 1:1; 1 Timothy 3:1-5; 2 Timothy 2:24; Hebrews 13:17)!

**The Bottom Line**

These principles will take time to learn, as they cut across what we may have learned in the marketplace, church, in your home and in life in general. Nevertheless, we are called to run life this way—His way. We can learn it and implement it! In so doing we will be excellent and successful in what really matters, serving by trusting and obeying our Lord Jesus Christ!

It is my prayer that as you read through these pages you will experience the real heart of God in your business, church and in your life. While you are reading this your tomorrow has already started, bring into it the heart of a Servant Leader.

**"Future intentions are determined by present action."**
**Blessings Phil.1:6**
**Rex Wolins**
**Optimum Leadership Consulting**
**www.optimumleadership.vpweb.com**

## CHAPTER
### I

*Core values / attributes or inward traits of the Everyday Optimum Leader*

## Core values / attributes or inward traits of the "Everyday Optimum Leader"

Some people sit and pontificate about whether leaders are made or born. The true leader ignores such arguments and instead concentrates on how to become better at leading people. We are going to discuss the leadership traits that people look for in a leader. If you are able to increase your skill in these traits, you will make it easier for people to want to follow you. The less time you have to spend on getting people to follow you, the more time you have to spend refining exactly where you want to go and how to get there.

Your skill at exhibiting these traits is strongly correlated with people's desire to follow your lead. Exhibiting these traits will inspire confidence in your leadership. Not exhibiting these traits or exhibiting the opposite of these traits will decrease your leadership influence with those around you.

It is important to exhibit these traits. Simply possessing each trait is not enough; you have to display it in a way that people notice. People want to see you demonstrating these traits—not just assuming that you have them. It isn't enough to just be neutral.

For example, just because you are not dishonest will not cause people to recognize that you are honest. Just avoiding displays of incompetence won't inspire the same confidence as truly displaying competence. The focus of each of these traits needs to be on what people see you do—not just the things they don't see you do. Being honest isn't a matter of not lying—it is taking the extra effort to display honesty.

### Honesty as a Leadership Trait

- Honesty—Display sincerity, integrity, and candor in all your actions. Deceptive behavior will not inspire trust.

People want to follow an honest leader. Years ago, many employees started out by assuming that their leadership was honest simply because the authority of their position. With modern scandals, this is no longer true. When you start a leadership position, you need to assume that people will think you are a little dishonest. In order to be seen as an honest individual, you will have to go out of your way to display honesty. People will not assume you are honest simply because you have never been caught lying.

One of the most frequent places where leaders miss an opportunity to display honesty is in handling mistakes. Much of a leader's job is to try new things and refine the ideas that don't work. However, many leaders want to avoid failure to the extent that they don't admit when something did not work. There was a medium size organization that was attempting to move to a less centralized structure. Instead of one location serving an entire city, they wanted to put smaller offices throughout the entire metro area. At the same time, they were planning an expansion for headquarters to accommodate more customers at the main site. The smaller remote offices was heralded as a way to reach more customers at a lower cost and cover more demographic areas.

After spending a considerable amount of money on a satellite location, it became clear that the cost structure would not support a separate smaller office. As the construction completed on the expanded headquarters building, the smaller office was closed. This was good decision making.

The smaller offices seemed like a good idea, but when the advantages didn't materialize (due to poor management or incorrect assumptions) it made sense to abandon the model.

This was a chance for the leadership to display honesty with the employees, be candid about why things didn't work out as expected, learn from the mistakes and move on. Unfortunately in this situation the leadership told employees that they had planned on closing the satellite location all along and it was just a temporary measure until construction was completed on the larger headquarters building. While this wasn't necessarily true, it didn't quite cross over into the area of lying.

Within a few months the situation was mostly forgotten and everyone moved on. Few of the employees felt that leadership was being dishonest. However, they had passed up a marvelous opportunity to display the trait of honesty in admitting a mistake.

Opportunities to display honesty on a large scale may not happen every day. As a leader, showing people that you are honest even when it means admitting to a mistake, displays a key trait that people are looking for in their leaders. By demonstrating honesty with yourself, with your organization and with outside organizations, you will increase your leadership influence. People will trust someone who actively displays honesty—not just as an honest individual, but as someone who is worth following.

## Forward-Looking as a Leadership Trait

*   Forward-looking Set goals and has a vision of the future. The vision must be owned throughout the organization. Effective leaders envision what they want and how to get it. They habitually pick priorities stemming from their basic values.

The whole point of leadership is figuring out where to go from where you are now. While you may know where you want to go, people won't see that unless you actively communicate it with them. Remember, these traits aren't just things you need to have, they are things you need to actively display to those around you. When people do not consider their leader forward-looking, that leader is usually suffering from one of two possible problems:

1.  The leader doesn't have a forward-looking vision.

2.  The leader is unwilling or scared to share the vision with others.

When a leader doesn't have a vision for the future, it usually because they are spending so much time on today, that they haven't really thought about tomorrow. On a very simplistic level this can be solved simply by setting aside some time for planning, strategizing and thinking about the future. Many times when a leader has no time to think and plan for the future, it is because they are doing a poor job of leading in the present. They have created an organization and systems that rely too much on the leader for input at every stage.

Some leaders have a clear vision, but don't wish to share it with others. Most of the time they are concerned that they will lose credibility if they share a vision of the future that doesn't come about. This is a legitimate concern. However, people need to know that a leader has a strong vision for the future and a strong plan for going forward. Leaders run into trouble sharing their vision of the future when they start making promises to individuals. This goes back to the trait of honesty. If a leader tells someone that "next year I'm going to make you manager of your own division", that may be a promise they can't keep. The leader is probably basing this promotion on the organization meeting financial goals, but the individual will only hear the personal promise.

I knew a man who worked in an organization that was floundering. It seemed like everyone had a different idea about what they were trying to achieve. Each department head was headed in a different direction and there was very little synergy as small fiefdoms and internal politics took their toll. Eventually a consulting firm was called in to help fix the problem. They analyzed the situation, talked to customers, talked to employees and set up a meeting with the CEO. They were going to ask him about his vision for the future. The employees were excited that finally there would be a report stating the direction for the organization.

After the meeting, the consultants came out shaking their heads. The employees asked how the important question had gone to which the consultants replied, "we asked him, but you aren't going to like the answer". The CEO had told the consultant that, while he had a vision and plan for the future, he wasn't going to share it with anyone because he didn't want there to be any disappointment if the goals were not reached. Leaders can communicate their goals and vision for the future without making promises that they may not be able to keep. If a leader needs to make a promise to an individual, it should be tied to certain measurable objectives being met. The CEO in the example didn't realize how much damage he was doing by not demonstrating the trait of being forward-looking by communicating his vision with the organization.

The CEO was forward-looking. He had a plan and a vision and he spent a lot of time thinking about where the organization was headed. However, his fear of communicating these things to the rest of the organization hampered his leadership potential.

## Competency as a Leadership Trait

* Competent—Your actions should be based on reason and moral principles. Do not make decisions based on childlike emotional desires or feelings.

People want to follow someone who is competent. This doesn't mean a leader needs to be the foremost expert on every area of the entire organization, but they need to be able to demonstrate competency. For a leader to demonstrate that they are competent, it isn't enough to just avoid displaying incompetency. Some people will assume you are competent because of your leadership position, but most will have to see demonstrations before deciding that you are competent. When people under your leadership look at some action you have taken and think, "that just goes to show why he is the one in charge", you are demonstrating competency. If these moments are infrequent, it is likely that some demonstrations of competency will help boost your leadership influence.

Like the other traits, it isn't enough for a leader to be competent. They must demonstrate competency in a way that people notice. This can be a delicate balance. There is a danger of drawing too much attention to yourself in a way that makes the leader seem arrogant. Another potential danger is that of minimizing others contributions and appearing to take credit for the work of others. As a leader, one of the safest ways to "toot you own horn without blowing it", is to celebrate and bring attention to team achievements. In this way you indirectly point out your competency as a leader.

## Inspiration as a Leadership Trait

- Inspiring—Display confidence in all that you do. By showing endurance in mental, physical, and spiritual stamina, you will inspire others to reach for new heights. Take charge when necessary.

People want to be inspired. In fact, there is a whole class of people who will follow an inspiring leader–even when the leader has no other qualities. If you have developed the other traits, being inspiring is usually just a matter of communicating clearly and with passion. Being inspiring means telling people how your organization is going to change the world. A great example of inspiration is when Steve Jobs stole the CEO from Pepsi by asking him, "Do you want to sell sugar water for the rest of your life, or do you want to change the world?" Being inspiring means showing people the big picture and helping them see beyond a narrow focus and understand how their part fits into the big picture.

One technique to develop your ability to inspire is telling stories. Stories that inspired you, examples from your customers, or even historical fables and myths. Stories can help you vividly illustrate what you are trying to communicate. Stories that communicate on an emotional level help communicate deeper than words and leave an imprint much stronger than anything you can achieve through a simple stating of the facts. Take note of people who inspire you and analyze the way they communicate. Look for ways to passionately express your vision. While there will always be room for improvement, a small investment in effort and awareness will give you a significant improvement in this leadership trait.

## Intelligence as a Leadership Trait

- Intelligent—Read, study, and seek challenging assignments. There is no substitute for doing your homework.

Intelligence is something that can be difficult to develop. The road toward becoming more intelligent is difficult, long and can't be completed without investing considerable time. Developing intelligence is a lifestyle choice. Your college graduation was the beginning of your education, not the end. In fact, much of what is taught in college functions merely as a foundational language for lifelong educational experiences. To develop intelligence you need to commit to continual learning–both formally and informally. With modern advances in distance, education it is easy to take a class or two each year from well respected professors in the evening at your computer.

Informally, you can develop a great deal of intelligence in any field simply by investing a reasonable amount of time to reading on a daily basis. The fact is that most people won't make a regular investment in their education. Spending 30 minutes of focused reading every day will give you 182 hours of study time each year. For the most part, people will notice if you are intelligent by observing your behavior and attitude. Trying to display your intelligence is likely to be counterproductive. One of the greatest signs of someone who is truly intelligent is humility. The greater your education, the greater your understanding of how little we really understand.

You can demonstrate your intelligence by gently leading people toward understanding–even when you know the answer. Your focus needs to be on helping others learn–not demonstrating how smart you are. Arrogance will put you in a position where people are secretly hopeful that you'll make a mistake and appear foolish. As unintuitive as it may seem, one of the best ways to exhibit intelligence is by asking questions. Learning from the people you lead by asking intelligent thoughtful questions will do more to enhance your intelligence credibility than just about anything. Of course this means you need to be capable of asking intelligent questions.

Everyone considers themselves intelligent. If you ask them to explain parts of their area of expertise and spend the time to really understand (as demonstrated by asking questions), their opinion of your intelligence will go up. After all, you now know more about what makes them so intelligent, so you must be smart as well. Your ability to demonstrate respect for the intellect of others will probably do more to influence the perception of your intellect than your actual intelligence.

### The Final three Leadership Traits

* Fair-minded—Show fair treatment to all people. Prejudice is the enemy of justice. Display empathy by being sensitive to the feelings, values, interests, and well being of others.

* Courageous—Have the perseverance to accomplish a goal, regardless of the seemingly insurmountable obstacles. Display a confident calmness when under stress.

* Imaginative—Make timely and appropriate changes in your thinking, plans, and methods. Show creativity by thinking of new and better goals, ideas, and solutions to problems. Be innovative!

### Summary of these Leadership Traits

By consciously making an effort to exhibit these traits, people will be more likely to follow you. These are the most important traits that people look for in their leaders. By exhibiting them on a regular basis, you will be able to grow your influence to its potential as an Everyday Optimum Leader.

**Attributes establish what leaders are,
and every leader needs at least three of them:**

### Standard Bearers

Establish the ethical framework within an organization. This demands a commitment to live and defend the climate and culture that you want to permeate your organization. What you set as an example will soon become the rule as unlike knowledge, ethical behavior is learned more by observing that by listening. And in fast moving situations, examples become certainty. Being a standard bearer creates trust and openness in your employees, who in turn, fulfill your **visions.**

## Developers

Help others learn through teaching, training, and coaching. This creates an exciting place to work and learn. Never miss an opportunity to teach or learn something new yourself. Coaching suggests someone who cares enough to get involved by encouraging and developing others who are less experienced. Employees who work for developers know that they can take risks, learn by making mistakes, and winning in the end.

## Integrators

Orchestrate the many activities that take place throughout an organization by providing a view of the future and the ability to obtain it. Success can only be achieved when there is a unity of effort. Integrators have a sixth sense about where problems will occur and make their presence felt during critical times. They know that their employees do their best when they are left to work within a vision-based framework.

These attributes are the very DNA or the core principals of, "Everyday Optimum Leadership."

In the final three leadership traits that we just talked about I would like to expand on the last one, and that is the excellent leadership trait of imagination.

## Imagination Creates Winning Teams

Imagination amplification and projection are on the top 5 list of a leader's priorities. A leader who can vividly imagine and then amp that vision and project it onto the hearts of others can create movements that change the world. A leader is a 'force multiplier' in that the leader multiplies the impact of her/his team in competition, battle, mission or business. You've seen it over and over again in sports, in business, where you work or go to school . . . when the leader shows up things happen. Sometimes they seem to happen almost 'magically.' It's as if, by their mere presence, a true leader amps the efforts of the team. They rise to new heights when the leader is in the huddle with them.

The leader carries several internal assets that make them a force multiplier. One of the assets that great leaders have is imagination and they usually have it in abundance. Not only do unusually great leaders possess great imaginations they also have a superior ability to project their vision so that it imprints the hearts of others and moves them into bold action.

1.  Read about and study great leaders like Jesus and learn how He imagined the future story for his followers and projected in a way that imprinted their hearts.

2.  Study leaders who have an uncanny ability to project their vision and practice doing the same. For example, pick up the book, "The Presentation Secrets of Steve Jobs" and study to see how you can improve your ability to project your imagination onto the hearts of others.

3.  Watch great movies and ask yourself how the movie production team 'projected' their imagination onto your heart and mind. Get more vivid in providing color, details, and even sound to your imagination projection. The more important your mission the harder you need to work on projection of your imagination. Begin with doing the hard work of imagining a Fantastic Future Story for you and your team and then practice projecting it with enough detail so that your listener's imaginations are vibrating in sync with yours.

4.  Learn historical leaders like Winston Churchill and Abraham Lincoln whose words galvanized their people to do whatever it would take to win against insurmountable odds.

5.  Watch great communicators who get action from their team. Study great preachers who get congregations to 'move' toward a grand vision. Watch great politicians who move people to action and see what you can learn. In short, become a student of leaders whose visions resonate with others because they have a vivid picture of preferred future story and they know how to project it in such a way that others respond. There is an art to being a great projector of vivid imaginations and there is not a more important art to master for a leader than this one. A couple of leaders that I study all the time are Andy Stanley of Northpoint Church near Atlanta, Georgia and Mark Batterson of National Community Church in Washington, D.C.

6.  Think. Take time to really think about your team & your cause and what it would look & feel like to 'win' in your context. What would it feel like to 'win'? Take time to process the challenges coming at you and your team and imagine solutions.

    Going to battle before you've consulted your advisors and imagined all the possible scenarios for winning (and the corollary, how you might get your butt kicked if you don't imagine proper solutions fully) is foolish. But, the Bible suggests that a wise man consults many advisors. I'd encourage you to think, imagine what it would take to win, practice projecting your vision with key leaders on your team and revise your mental imagery/projection based on their feedback.

    Then do it again and again as long as you have time so that you'll be fully ready to project your teams future story in a vivid, compelling fashion and your brain will have rehearsed enough possible different outcomes that you can flex and fly as things change. It's not so much that your plan has to work as imagined, but that you, your brain, and your collective 'team brain' have worked your imaginations to the point where you can readily make wise decisions on the fly that lead to the preferred outcome of 'winning')

7.  Hash it out. As you're thinking capture your thoughts in an easy to manipulate fashion so that you can sequence your thinking for clear

projection later. In the beginning it's enough to just get your brain emptied of 'stuff' and that you capture your brain dump as you move along.

Once the brain dump is complete you can start to sequence the information so that it will make sense to others and can be properly 'projected' via print, in person, via talks and speeches, video, blogs . . . whatever. You want your message to be so crystal clear that it projects vivid powerful images onto the hearts of others. Imagination is 98% perspiration and the willingness to think about your teams preferred future story. The other 2% comes from talents and gifts that you may have as a communicator. But, even a nominal communicator with a powerful vision that has been thought through, hashed out, rehearsed and rehashed will win over a great communicator who has not been disciplined in preparing to project a compelling future for his or her team.

This morning I heard a news story on Fox News about the Mumbai Massacre in India last year. The person being interviewed said that the terrorists 'out-imagined' the police and the civil authorities.

That was a powerful reminder to me as a leader to continually re-imagine the future and re-project it over and over to our team so that when the chips are down that we won't be 'out-imagined' by a competitor or by a shift in the marketplace. Your Leadership Style has its roots in your internal Leadership operating system, that is, your internalized leadership theory. And, your leadership theory is propelled by your internal visualization of what's possible and what you as a leader can do.

So, down in the heart of your Personal Leadership Operating System you have an imagination about what a leader is, about what a leader does, about what's possible as a leader and about what's possible as a team.

So, it's important to fire up your imagination machine and to fuel it with powerful possibilities so that your ability to lead is amped and your leadership style and leadership theory is cranked up to the max for who you are and what your team needs from you today. A leader's internal vision is the well-spring of the leader's operating system and that operating system is governed by the onboard theory of leadership the leader packs around. The style of the leader can be enhanced dramatically by mentally rehearsing how great historical leaders would deal with the challenges at hand.

For every great leader who wants to have a broader theory base and a wider range of operational leadership styles imagination is their greatest asset to generate change.

# CHAPTER
## II

*Practice makes <u>perfect</u> = Mature*

**All five practices work together** reflecting a synergy that is true to the essence of the servant as leader. It makes for an exciting journey. Study carefully this visual (expanded from the introduction), beginning to assess key elements of your pattern of Servant Leadership:

**Practice #1 Empowered Leadership**

**"Doing the right things in His power."** The presence, power, and pattern of Christ empower us to follow Him as servant leaders; that is the starting place.

**Glossary—empower:** *To invest with power, especially legal power or official authority. To equip or supply with an ability; to enable. Usage Note: Although it is a contemporary buzzword, "empower" arose in the mid-17th century with the legalistic meaning "to invest with authority, to authorize." Shortly thereafter it began to be used with an infinitive in a more general way meaning "to enable or permit." These uses survive today, overpowered by its use in politics and pop psychology.*—from <u>The American Heritage® Dictionary of English Language</u>, Fourth Edition:

**Christ Himself is the "big picture" for all who would practice Servant Leadership.**

He is the one who has given us authority to move forward to engage in kingdom work (Matt. 28:18). Chart your course to follow Him. He is the largest window of opportunity, inclusive of Servant Leadership, the most powerful source of our energy, the truest example/model for every follower. *"He is the starter and finisher of faith . . ."* (See Heb. 12:1-2). (NKJV)

**Hebrews 12:1-2**

*We are to run this race "with no eyes for anyone or anything except Jesus" (Moffatt, in loc.). It is He toward whom we run. There must be no divided attention. The "author and perfecter of faith" (there is no "our" in the Gr.) may mean that Jesus trod the way of faith first and brought it to completion.*

19

*Or it may mean that He originated His people's faith and will bring it to its perfection.*—Zondervan Commentary

His **abiding presence in our lives fashions who we are as followers/servants** (See John 15:9).

**John 15:9**—*Love is the relationship that unites the disciples to Christ as branches are united to a vine. Two results stem from this relationship: obedience and joy. Obedience marks the cause of their fruitfulness; joy is its result.*—Zondervan Commentary

He sets the ideal pattern for Servant Leadership in Christian ministry (see 1 John 2:6). "What would Jesus do?" is more than a popular bracelet; it is the energizing standard.

**John 2:6**—*The uniqueness of Christian ethics comes again to the surface. Relationship to God requires moral behavior worthy of God. And as the revelation of God in Christ is accepted as the high point of divine self-disclosure, so the human life of Jesus becomes the measuring stick of true moral and ethical behavior.*—Zondervan Commentary.

Union with Christ is the source for all the tasks, functions and challenges of Christian ministry (John 15:5).

**John 15:5**—*Fruit bearing is not only possible but certain if the branch remains in union with the vine. Uniformity of quantity and quality are not promised. But if the life of Christ permeates a disciple, fruit will be inevitable.*—Zondervan Commentary

Practice **what Jesus did;** the disciplines and practices we find in the life and servant leadership of Christ, we should choose for ourselves.

For example:

Pray as Jesus prayed . . . (see Luke 11:1-4)
Love as Jesus loved . . . (see John 13:34-35)

Walk as Jesus walked . . . (see 1 John 2:5-6)
Obey as Jesus obeyed . . . (see John 15:9-14)
Care as Jesus cared . . . (see Luke 10:29-35)
Work as Jesus worked . . . (John 9:4-5)
Send as Jesus sent . . . (John 3:16-17)
Lead as Jesus led . . . (see Mark 10:43-45)

**Jesus is our Way in His service** E. Stanley Jones, veteran missionary, passed down an account of a missionary who lost his way in an African jungle—no landmark, no trail. Finally coming upon a native's hut, he asked if he could lead him out. The native arose, walked into the bush and for hours hacked his way forward. The concerned missionary finally asked: "Are you sure this is the way? I don't see any path." The African chuckled over his shoulder, "Bwana, in this place there is no path. I am the path." (Source: www.bible.org/illes/1.1-20.htm)

**Seven ways Jesus empowers servant leaders:**

**Seven contemporary terms,** among those prevalent today, can be used to describe how Jesus was "the Master" at empowering His followers to be servant leaders: authority, acceptance, affirmation, delegation, enablement, encouragement, and support.

**Seven biblical realities,** often expressed in the ministry of Jesus, empower 1st century and contemporary servant leaders: indwelling of the Holy Spirit; enduring truth of Holy Scripture; calling to vocation, to ministry; spiritual giftedness; kingdom mission; and seeking and doing the will of God.

**Practice #2 Ethical Leadership**

**"Doing the right things for the right reasons."** Servant Leadership asks and seeks to answer the ethical questions: "Why am I serving this way, or leading in that manner?" "What is the true motivation and outcome of my life and leadership?" "Am I following biblical character and principles?" In public and corporate life, ethical responsibility is so critical.

**Glossary—ethical:** *Conforming to accepted standards of social or professional behavior; adhering to ethical and moral principles; "it seems ethical and right."*—WordNet ® 1.6 © 1997 Princeton University

*"Always do right. This will gratify some people and astonish the rest."*—Mark Twain

**The centerpiece for ethical leadership** for Christian ministers and Christians in general, in every role or position, is shaped by the example of Jesus Christ and His indwelling life presence (John 15:5-8); and the guidance of the Spirit (John 16:12-13).

**Love is the ethical mandate** Christ has given to each of us. If the Sermon on the Mount (Matthew 5-7) serves as an ethical pattern for those practicing servant leadership, then love is its ethical core.

*You have heard that it was said, 'Love your neighbor and hate your enemy.' But I tell you: Love your enemies and pray for those who persecute you, . . .*—Matt. 5:43-44

**Servant leaders should** seek and follow ethical instructions given throughout Holy Scripture; examples:

**Luke 6:31**—*Do to others as you would have them do to you.*

**Matt. 22:37-40**—*Jesus replied: "Love the Lord your God with all your heart and with all your soul and with all your mind." This is the first and greatest commandment. And the second is like it: "Love your neighbor as yourself. All the Law and the Prophets hang on these."*

**Deut. 10:11-13**—*"Go," the Lord said to me, "and lead the people on their way, so that they may enter and possess the land that I swore to their fathers to give them." And now, O Israel, what does the Lord your God ask of you but to fear the Lord your God, to walk in all his ways, to love him, to serve the Lord your God with all your heart and with all your soul, and to observe the Lord's commands and decrees that I am giving you today for your own good?*

**Authentic "lived-in" character is the fabric of servant-first leadership.**

**Integrity has come to be the most sought-after characteristic** of leaders in all areas of life; how much more within the sphere of servant-followers of Christ.

**Honesty was ranked the highest among the characteristics** expected of superior leaders, before any skill or competence. This is true in national and international studies, insisting that there must be a consistency between words and deeds. (See Kouzes and Posner, The Leadership Challenge, pp. 16-17.)

**Ethical leaders follow a "moral compass."** Ultimately we judge our ministry leaders in a framework of biblical values. In society, "morality refers to the standards by which a community judges the rightness and wrongness of conduct in all fields" (Gardner, On Leadership, p. 76).

*He has showed you, O man, what is good. And what does the Lord require of you? To act justly and to love mercy and to walk humbly with your God.—* Micah 6:8

**The "best test" of servant leadership**, according to Robert Greenleaf, is an ethical threshold for us all.

*The best test is: Do those served grow as persons? Do they, while being served become healthier, wiser, freer, more autonomous, more likely themselves to become servants? And, what is the effect on the least privileged in society; will they benefit, or, at least, not be further deprived?—*Robert K. Greenleaf, Servant Leadership, pp. 13-14

Servant Leadership does not merely pursue achievements, or results, or position, or recognition—by any means. Applied to the public arena, the servant leader seeks to contribute to the common good and the improvement of individual persons. Ethical leadership includes using authority and power for service to others—not for self-service. Leaders should specify what their goals are for the group and what they consider right—and why. (See also Gardner, p. 73.)

## An ethical leadership checklist might include questions such as:

Is it right: is it true to biblical standards?

Is it the best: does it measure up to the example of Christ?

Is it fair: are people treated equitably?

Is it legal: does it violate civil law?

Is it approved: is it permitted by church policies?

Is it best for the long-term, the system?

How will you feel later, if it were to be published and read by others?

What if others did this: if done by all, how would it contribute to the common good?

## Practice #3 Enabling Leadership

**"Doing the right things together."** Servant leadership builds relationships, enriches congregational fellowship, and develops the life and competence of fellow workers in the marketplace.

**Glossary—enabling:** *To supply with the means, knowledge, or opportunity; make able: techniques that enable surgeons to open and repair the heart. To make feasible or possible.*—from The American Heritage® Dictionary of the English Language, Fourth Edition

**Leadership is within the company of others,** not a solo performance. In fact, one test of a leader is "to look over your shoulder to see if anyone is following."

Leadership is first a trusting, team relationship; then it can move toward performance and contribution. Servant-first leaders practice open communication, mutual respect, and works for the common good.

Full participation in the body of Christ offers opportunities to learn and develop as an individual and team member; opportunities to risk and fail and learn; genuine caring for people as people (not just assets for ministry); and, experience the congregation as a family/social system.

**Servant leadership is an equipping ministry** as set out in Ephesians 4:11-13. Equipping others enables them to become servants and matures them toward leadership and may be described by a diversity of tasks:

*It was he who gave some to be apostles, some to be prophets, some to be evangelists, and some to be pastors and teachers, to prepare God's people for works of service, so that the body of Christ may be built up . . .—Ephesians 4:11-12*

Equipped, strengthened, fitted, readied, prepared, approved, commissioned, delegated, entrusted, built-up, edified, developed, competent, skilled, talented, motivated, encouraged.

**Enabling leadership builds on the "one another connection" of the New Testament witness.** The following Scriptures affirm that we are servants of one another; dependent on one another and commissioned to do Christ's work together:

John 13:34—*"so you must love one another."* (See also Jn. 15:12, 17; Rom. 13:8; 1 Jn. 3:11; 4:7)
Rom. 12:5—*"each member belongs to all the others."*
Rom. 12:10—*"Honor one another above yourselves."*
Rom. 12:16—*"Live in harmony with one another."*
Rom. 12:18—*"live at peace with everyone."* (Mk. 9:50; Rom. 14:19)
Rom. 14:13—*"stop passing judgment on one another."*
Rom. 15:7—*"Accept one another."*
1 Cor. 12:25—*"have equal concern for each other."*
Gal. 5:13—*"serve one another in love."*
Gal. 6:2—*"Carry each other's burdens."*
Eph. 4:32—*"Be kind and compassionate to one another."*
1 Thess. 5:11—*"Therefore encourage one another."* (Heb. 3:13)
1 Thess. 5:11—*"build each other up."* (Heb. 3:13)

James 5:16—*"confess your sins to each other."*
James 5:16—*"pray for each other."*
1 John 1:7—*"we have fellowship with one another."*

## Practice #4 Effective Leadership

**"Doing the right things on purpose."** Servant leaders intentionally seek to establish kingdom mission, goals, and direction with the church body, its members and in the marketplace. That is the mark of effectiveness or excellence Paul sought in the service of Christ:

**2 Tim. 2:15**—*Do your best to present yourself to God as one approved, a workman who does not need to be ashamed and who correctly handles the word of truth.*

**Phil. 3:12-14**—*Not that I have already obtained all this, or have already been made perfect, but I press on to take hold of that for which Christ Jesus took hold of me. Brothers, I do not consider myself yet to have taken hold of it. But one thing I do: Forgetting what is behind and straining toward what is ahead, I press on toward the goal to win the prize for which God has called me heavenward in Christ Jesus.*

1. **Personal effectiveness:** Commit yourself to a lifetime of growth, development, and contribution:

Continue to learn about your service/leadership roles—from Scripture, studies, experience, mentors, and ministry team members. Covey, Habit #7—*"Sharpen the saw is the endowment of continuous improvement or self-renewal to overcome entropy"* (Principle-Centered Leadership, p. 47). He also admonishes: *"Think **effectiveness** with people; **efficiency** with things and methods"* (p. 52).

Discover and put into practice your **spiritual gifts**, empowering you to work with others to pursue kingdom goals.

**Romans 12:8**— . . . *if it is leadership, let him govern diligently; . . . Actually exercise consistently your giftedness, what you have learned, and the skills developed.*

Personal effectiveness has a diverse set of traits and skills; examples only include:

A personal sense of mission and calling, high regard and respect for others, integrity in behavior and methods, communication skills, with a focus on listening, forward-looking, visionary, intelligence, job knowledge, energy for "second mile" efforts.

**Congregational effectiveness:** In church or the marketplace work with your congregation or team to establish and achieve kingdom goals.

In the church think about the congregation as a **social/spiritual** "system"; the connectedness of the parts affect the whole. Do not be shortsighted or crisis/event driven. Establish with the congregation a kingdom-size mission/vision as its true center. Assess its actual situation, its opportunities, challenges, and resources. Cast the mission/vision into a desired future.

In the marketplace empower the coworkers to transform vision into a new reality; implement toward desired results with objectives, goals, and action plans. Effective leaders consistently develop as servant leaders; and, they consistently work with others to pursue kingdom purposes.

**James H. Landes: A Model of Servant Leadership:**

**Tribute**

James H. Landes—pastor, executive, visionary, put together a simple model regarding Servant Leadership. Here are the core items of that model. Respect individuals and individuality. Develop those who work with you to their full potential. Develop a sense of gratitude; be gentle and caring in your relationship with others. Keep structures that permit change and renewal. Live your life fully motivated by the cross of Jesus Christ; seek to know the will of God for your life and work. Learn all you can about the institutions, churches, associations, etc. Constructive criticism in the marketplace is in order. Make judgments knowing that your judgments are only approximations of the whole. Prevent dry-rot in the workplace: search for the right people; develop open, healthy environment and communications. Provide for self-criticism; build it into the process; know and accept yourself. Be more interested in what is going to be rather than in what has been; live with purpose. Love: first, last, in every way—love.

## Practice #5 Efficient Leadership

**"Doing the right things in the right way."** Servant leadership competently organizes and administers ministries and tasks toward the support of kingdom mission and goals. "Management" and skill development are not unimportant disciplines—they are a must in a serving church or business.

**There is no single word in the Bible translated "efficient,"** but . . .

There are several words carrying that concept of **"efficiency"**: order, orderly, manage, administration, stewardship, and others. Our own vocabulary has a plethora of such terms: able, capable, useful, accomplished, competent, practiced, fitted, "handy," even well organized.

**Competence:** Beyond any doubt, the fundamental way to be a servant leader is to do well whatever tasks, function, or role you offer as a follower of Christ.

**Administration:** 1 Cor. 12:28—"those with gifts of administration" (from the word to steer, steerage, one who is a steersman, a pilot). The word indicates proofs of ability to hold a leading position in the church. Some are gifted by the Spirit to lead the church body to organize its ministries and resources to move together toward the larger purpose. In 2 Cor. 8:20-21, Paul described the careful way he and others administered the generous gift for the Jerusalem poor; efficiency implemented the mission.

**Stewardship:** probably the NT word most like "management" or "administration," meaning one who has charge over the affairs of others:

Luke 16:2—*"Give an account of your management."*
Luke 12:42—*"Who then is the faithful and wise manager?"*
1 Cor. 4:2—*"it is required of stewards that one be found faithful."*

**Management:** is expressed in the NT by two different words—both used in 1 Tim. 3:1-5: One who desires to be an "overseer" (*episkopos*) must be above reproach: one who looks carefully for, who considers, a watchman. One who demonstrates he is able to take care of God's church by "managing" well his own family: one who is set over, who stands before, who has charge of.

**Order(ly)** is a term in the NT that emphasizes order, disciplined arrangement, organization:

Titus 1:5—Paul reminded Titus that he was left on the isle of Crete to "set in order" and finish the work. 1 Cor. 14:40—In the midst of spiritual gifts and church worship, Paul told the church that *"everything should be done in a fitting and orderly way."*

**Management leadership within the congregation or business** may be guided by the few but is implemented by many individuals and teams. There are typical roles and tasks such as:

Communications, planning/organizing, budgeting/controlling, allocating resources supervising/directing, training/development, office procedures, building management evaluating/assessing.

## Robert Greenleaf: Ten Characteristics of the Servant-Leader

The following ten characteristics of servant-leadership are abstracted from Reflections on Leadership, *"Introduction: Servant-Leadership and The Greenleaf Legacy"* (p. 4-7) by Larry Spears, who is editor of the book. Larry Spears, executive director of the Greenleaf Center for Servant Leadership, quotes from the <u>New York Times</u>: *Servant leadership deals with the reality of power in everyday life—its legitimacy, the ethical restraints upon it and the beneficial results that can be attained through the appropriate use of power.*

## Ten Critical Characteristics of the Servant-Leader:

**Listening:** Although leaders have been valued for their communication and decision-making skills, servant-leaders must reinforce these important skills by listening intently to others.

**Empathy:** Servant-leaders strive to understand and empathize with others, and to accept and recognize people for their special and unique spirits.

**Healing:** Learning to heal one's self and others is a powerful force for transformation, integration, and healing the brokenhearted.

**Awareness:** General awareness, and especially self-awareness, strengthens the servant-leader; it also aids in understanding issues involving ethics and values.

**Persuasion:** Servant-leaders rely upon persuasion, rather than positional authority. In making decisions within an organization, they seek to convince others rather than coerce compliance.

**Conceptualization:** Servant-leaders seek to nurture their abilities to "dream great dreams"; to encompass broader-based conceptual thinking; and to articulate these to others.

**Foresight:** The ability to foresee likely outcomes of a situation is hard to define, but includes understanding lessons from the past, realities of the present and likely consequences of a decision for the future.

**Stewardship:** By "holding something in trust for another," servant-leadership—like stewardship—assumes first and foremost a commitment to serving the needs of others.

**Commitment to the growth of people:** People have an intrinsic value beyond their tangible contributions as workers; as such, servant-leaders are deeply committed to their own personal, professional, and spiritual growth, and especially to the young.

**Building community:** Servant-leaders seek to identify and demonstrate building true community among those who work within a given institution; institutions need our caring.

# CHAPTER
## III

*Making an Optimum Decision*

# Decision-Making: Process and Tools

## *"A Ten-Step Process with Tools"*

**Note: Decision-making is a process.**

This describes a ten-step process including spiritual and mental preparation. Decision-making also involves action. Unless some action results, a decision has not really been made. Implementation of the decision is an important part of the process, and this concept deals with that also.

**Objective:** To present the decision-making process, along with useful tools, so that the leader can apply it effectively to daily issues of life and leadership.

**Solomon:** *So give your servant a discerning heart to govern your people and to distinguish between right and wrong. For who is able to govern this great people of yours?*—1 Kings 3:9

## What Are the Different Kinds of Decisions?

Not all decisions are alike, and, of course, the process to be used. The kind of decision to be made will in some measure determine the process to be followed. Some decisions are personal and made by an individual; others are made in a group process, either a small group or a large one. These ten-steps specifically address each of these kinds of decisions. Some decisions are major or life changing. The most important is trusting Christ as Savior and Lord. Other so-called major decisions include deciding whom to marry (or if), what occupation to follow, where to live, and what friends to have.

Some decisions are more or less routine, such as what clothes to wear to work or what route to take to a friend's house. However, these "routine" decisions can sometimes become life-changing decisions. Thus, all decisions should be given consideration, although not all take the same amount of time and thought to process. What kind of decisions are you now dealing with? Here are some other different kinds of decisions: optional and compulsory; "whether" and "which"; simple and complex; preferences and priorities; tastes and values; controversial and uncontroversial; crisis and routine; right or wrong.

## Decision-Making Process—for You

Realize the vital importance of decisions and learn all you can as a Christian servant leader about making better decisions. As you make decisions, follow the basic steps in decision-making, avoiding the common pitfalls along the way.

**Make your own decision-making process, step by step, one that you can follow consistently.** This is an overview of decision-making from a Christian perspective for the servant leader. **Note:** Review the graph as you work through this series.

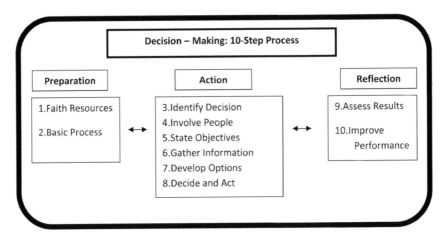

| Decision – Making: 10-Step Process | | |
|---|---|---|
| **Preparation** | **Action** | **Reflection** |
| 1. Faith Resources<br>2. Basic Process | 3. Identify Decision<br>4. Involve People<br>5. State Objectives<br>6. Gather Information<br>7. Develop Options<br>8. Decide and Act | 9. Assess Results<br>10. Improve Performance |

## Decision-Making: Fast Track Process

You may prefer to keep your process very simple, especially for short, quick, less systemic decisions. Consider this fast-track as a mental checklist for such decisions:

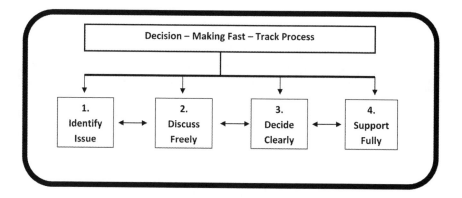

## Reflection and Application

Review this process several times.

Rewrite the process if it doesn't work for you.

Put it on a 3x5 laminated card.

Use it as an on-the-spot checklist for your bigger decisions.

## *"Step One—Draw upon Christian Faith Resources"*

What contributions to decision-making does the Christian faith make? Christians ought to begin the decision-making process with a faith commitment that God not only exists but that He is sovereign and has a will and purpose for each person as well as for all groups and relationships.

## God is the ultimate authority in decision-making.

Secular approaches look to reason, enlightened self-interest, social standards, or perhaps law. Though intelligently considering these, the Christian approach looks to God with a firm belief that God's will is always best and good. *"And we know that in all things God works for the good of those who love him, who have been called according to his purpose."*—Rom. 8:10 (NIV)

## Soul competency/making choices

Christians also believe that God makes His will known to those who are open to seek and receive it. Furthermore, Christians believe that persons are capable (or competent) of knowing and following God's will. Baptists and others term this capability as "soul competency" and cherish the concept. Closely related is the conviction that each person who responds by faith to Jesus Christ as Savior and Lord becomes a **believer priest** with opportunity to know God directly and with responsibility to put that knowledge into action in life and ministry.

The Bible is filled with illustrations and teachings indicating that persons are capable of knowing God's will and are responsible for carrying it out. (See for example, Prov. 3:21, 31; Isa. 7:15; 2 Cor. 9:6-8; James 4:4.) One of the most dramatic statements in the Bible along these lines is that of Joshua to the people of Israel: *"Now fear the Lord and serve him with all faithfulness . . . . But if serving the Lord seems undesirable to you, then choose for yourselves this day whom you will serve, whether the gods your forefathers served beyond the River, or the gods of the Amorites, in whose land you are living. But as for me and my household, we will serve the Lord"*—Joshua 24:14-15 (NIV). Day by day, we must each choose whom we will serve. The Christian decision maker chooses on the basis of being a servant of God.

### Willing to know God's will

Jesus taught that we must be willing to know God's will (John 7:17). Such willingness grows out of our closeness to God, out of worship and love for God. The human landscape is littered with the tragic consequences of persons making decisions when they were spiritually cold. *"The first indicator of good decision-making is that we have made our decision not in moments of self-doubt, but in moments of worshiping the living God."*—<u>The Empowered Leader</u>, Miller, p. 86 Jesus also indicated that no one perfectly knows or carries out God's will (Matthew 19:17), except of course Jesus Himself. No one has a "hot line" to God and can claim perfect insight into His will. Why?—because as humans we are finite, sinful, corrupted by our society, and prone to self-delusion and rationalization.

**Christians are indeed provided resources** that are specifically designed for those who have faith commitment to God—among these are God Himself, the life and teachings of Jesus, the guidance and empowerment of the Holy Spirit, and the Bible.

**God Himself is the source of wisdom;** James wrote, *"If any of you lacks wisdom, he should ask God, who gives generously to all without finding fault, and it will be given to him."* (James 1:5)

**Jesus in His teachings provides the basic values that are to guide decisions.** For example, He taught that we are to love God, neighbor, and self (Matthew 22:37-40) and that we are to seek first the Kingdom of God and His righteousness (Matthew 6:33), and that His way is that of servant. (Mark 10:42-45)

**The Holy Spirit is one of God's gifts to servant leaders** to aid in decision-making. Jesus said, *"But when he, the Spirit of truth, comes, he will guide you into all truth . . . ."* (John 16:13)

**The decision of the early church** about the place of Gentiles in the churches is an example of the role of the Holy Spirit in decision-making. In drafting the decision to share with others, the members of the church in Jerusalem wrote: *"It seems good to the Holy Spirit and to us not to burden you with anything beyond the following requirements: . . ."* (Acts 15:28, NIV)

**The Bible provides indispensable help** to the servant leader in decision-making. The Bible does not contain answers for all decisions we face, but it does provide guidelines and examples to aid us in making decisions. For example, the life of Moses recorded in the Bible illustrates that some decisions can and ought to be delegated; we do not have to make all decisions on our own (Exodus 18:13-27). The Bible provides many examples of both good and bad decisions and the consequences of each. *"Because we will be wrong sometimes, we should be thankful for God's grace and forgiveness and learn to forgive ourselves. Ability in decision making can be improved by study and practice."*—Pinson, <u>Ready to Minister</u>, p. 86

Even with these resources Christian servant leaders do not always follow the best process or arrive at the best choice in decision-making. Because we are prone to fail to find and follow God's will in decision-making, we ought to be profoundly grateful for God's forgiveness and grace. Knowledge of God's grace frees us to plunge ahead in decision-making, doing our best to discover God's way and accepting our limitations in doing so. *"No one can serve two masters. Either he will hate the one and love the other, or he will be devoted to the one and despise the other. You cannot serve both God and Money."*—Mt. 6:24 (NIV)

### *"Step Two—Follow a Basic Decision Process"*

1. **Benefits of a Basic Process for Making Decisions**—A process for making decisions is better than a haphazard, hit-and-miss approach. Because most persons have not had the benefit of a careful study of decision-making, many lack such a process. Hopefully, out of this study you will develop your own systematic process. *Experts in decision-making point out that a systematic approach helps you to:*

   *Address the right decision problem*
   *Clarify your real objectives*
   *Develop a range of creative alternatives*
   *Understand the consequences of your decision*
   *Make appropriate tradeoffs among conflicting objectives*
   *Deal sensibly with uncertainties*
   *Take account of your risk-taking attitude*
   *Plan ahead for decisions linked over time*

2. **Criteria for the Basic Process**—Regardless of the kind of decision to be made, certain steps are deemed important to arrive at a good decision. These steps may be taken subconsciously or very deliberately, informally or formally, but in any case each is important. The amount of time, thought, and energy given to a decision will vary; the basic steps should not.

And what are these steps? Authorities in decision-making differ as to which ones are absolutely essential and how to name or describe each step. Whatever process or steps a person may follow, an effective decision-making process will fulfill these six criteria:

   *It focuses on what is important.*
   *It is logical and consistent.*
   *It acknowledges both subjective and objective factors and blends analytical with intuitive thinking.*
   *It requires only as much information and analysis as is necessary to resolve a particular dilemma.*

*It encourages and guides the gathering of relevant information and informed opinion.*

*It is straightforward, reliable, easy to use, and flexible.*

**3. To these the Christian servant leader will add:**

It begins with a faith commitment in God.

It utilizes the resources available to the follower of Jesus Christ.

It is consistent with the life and teaching of Jesus Christ.

It seeks to advance the purposes of the kingdom of God.

Some authorities on decision-making endeavor to reduce the process to a formula or easily memorized summary. This approach is represented by the following, labeled the PROACT approach:

**PR**oblem

**O**bjectives

**A**lternatives

**C**onsequences

**T**radeoffs

Uncertainty

Risk Tolerance

Linked Decisions

**4. Most agree that the following are important to the decision-making process**, each of which is included in the above "formula":

- Recognize the need for a decision.
- Determine if this decision really needs to be made.
- Identify the persons who should make the decision—individual, if so, whom; group, if so, which—and the person or group to assign the decision-making responsibility.
- Understand the nature of the decision and/or problem.
- State the objectives or priorities involved in the decision.
- Gain opinions about the options or alternatives.
- Obtain facts and information related to the decision.

- Identify the boundary conditions related to the decision.
- State clearly the options or alternatives.
- Evaluate the options or alternatives.
- Make a tentative decision and assess it.
- Make the final decision and announce or publicize it.
- Implement the decision.
- Assess the impact of the decision and monitor the results.
- Analyze the process used in making the decision and see what can be learned in order to improve the decision-making process.

### Step Three—"Identify a Basic Decision Process" and
### Step Four—"Involve the Right People"

## Step Three

Recognize **the Need for a Decision**—When should the decision-making process be initiated? Basically, whenever a problem or issue occurs that calls for determining what course of action is best to deal with it or when a person confronts alternative courses of action and needs to determine which is the best (or better) to take.

Author and Philosopher Wilfred A. Peterson says, *"Decision is the courageous facing of issues, knowing that if they are not faced, problems will remain forever unanswered."*—Bethel, p. 149

**Life consists of a steady stream of problems or alternatives clamoring for choices** to be made. Some of these may appear to be "no brainers." For example, the outside temperature is forty below zero. Should I wear an overcoat? Most alternatives are not that simple to choose between, however. Even what appear to be very minor decisions, such as whether to order a salad or not in a cafeteria line, cause some people to undergo a "panic attack"—and the persons behind them in the line to grow ever more irritated. **A single choice of food may be no big deal.** However, a pattern of choices can lead to good health or disaster. When confronted with alternative courses of action, each should be taken seriously; although, in many cases the importance of the choice does not warrant a full-blown, formal, conscious decision-making process.

**Determine if This Decision Really Needs To Be Made.** Keep in mind that a decision to make no decision is actually a decision. Failure to acknowledge and deal with a problem likely will cause it only to become worse. However, sometimes a problem is best left unattended. No one can solve all the problems of life. Some problems may just take care of themselves.

**When confronted by a number of decisions prioritize.** Determine which ones are more important. Unfortunately, often those that appear most urgent are not the most important. Some refer to this as the "tyranny of the urgent." You can find yourself so mired in minor but urgent decisions that you never get to the major ones. Also, most of us have **a tendency to put off tough choices in favor of easy ones,** and this contributes to majoring on minors in decision-making. Of course, procrastination also plays a role for many . . . putting off until tomorrow what you could do today.

How do you determine which decisions ought to be tackled? Which are the really important ones in a mix of decisions? That is tough to answer and depends on many factors. However, if a person has his or her overall values and goals clearly in mind (a personal or organizational mission and value statement will help), then those decisions are most important that either serve to greatly advance or horribly hinder reaching those goals or abiding by those values. Isn't it ironic that early in the decision-making process you are called on to **make a decision about which decision to deal with**? But that's the way it is.

**Understand the Nature of the Decision**. Once the decision-making is in the appropriate hands, the next step is for the person or group to determine what the nature of the decision really is. For example, is this a "whether" decision—should various courses of action be examined?; or a "which" decision—which of several possibilities should be chosen? A case in point would be a person dealing with marriage possibilities. One decision would be a "whether" decision—whether to marry. Or it might be a "which" decision (or in this case "whom")—of various persons, which one is the "right" one?

*You can make a well-considered, well-thought-out decision, but if you've started from the wrong place—with the wrong decision problem—you won't have made the smart choice. The way you state your problem frames your decision. It determines the alternatives you consider and the way you evaluate them. Posing the right problem drives everything else.*

As much as possible, frame the nature of the decision in a positive way. Look at the decision more as an opportunity than a problem (even though it may be a problem!). By wording the decision in a positive way, the outcome is likely to be more positive and more readily accepted.

## *Step Four*

<u>Identify</u> **the Person or Persons Who Should Make the Decision.** Even if you assess that a decision needs to be made, you are not necessarily the person to make it. If not you, then who? Who is responsible for this decision? That depends on the nature of the decision. If it is a decision that calls for individual rather than group decision-making, these questions might help: Who is most qualified to deal with this matter? Who has the time available to deal with it? Who has the biggest stake in the correct decision? If you are not the best person to deal with the decision, you will need to determine how to enlist the appropriate decision-maker.

**Usually the person who is most responsible** or who will be the most efficient in implementing the decision ought to be the decision-maker. In other words, those closest to the problem likely will be the choice to deal with it. But this is not always true. Sometimes a person may be so involved in the problem that he/she cannot deal with it objectively. Keep these factors in mind: **"Upward delegation"** often exists in an organization; persons in a structure may try to pass the decision-making buck back to the person who assigned it to them. A **"gung ho"** member of an organization may take on decisions that he or she is not really equipped to deal with—either because that is his or her nature or because he or she desires to please or make a name for himself or herself.

If the decision calls for **group action**, then someone must determine which group. In an organization, the structure of the organization may well determine the group. For example, in a church if a staff member is causing serious problems and the pastor or staff leader has been unable to resolve the matter, then the **personnel or some appropriate standing committee** likely is the appropriate group to decide what to do. If no group is the routine choice, then the leader of the organization must make the decision as to the group to deal with the decision.

**Decisions! Decisions!** Even before you get to the actual process of dealing with a specific decision, there are decisions to make—like who is to be involved.

### Step Five—"State the Guiding Objectives and Priorities" and Step Six—"Gather Decision-Making Information"

## Step Five

State the Objectives or the Priorities That Will Guide the Decision-Making Process—Clearly stating objectives means thinking through what you really want to accomplish by this decision; that is, what is vital and of ultimate importance. The objectives or goals should be in keeping with your basic values, such as love for God and neighbor and seeking first the Kingdom of God. Thus, if a stated objective is selfish and serves only to advance your own desires, it is out of line and needs to be reworked.

**Case of buying a house.** Consider objectives that might be listed for the purchase of a home, for example. A person might list an objective such as "luxurious enough to establish status and success." This objective will determine many other factors, such as what facts are sought about houses and neighborhood. However, do these objectives fit with basic values for a follower of Christ? Another person might list as an objective in deciding about a house to purchase: "Overall cost leaves adequate funds for contributions to Christian charity." With this objective, a different set of facts will be gathered concerning houses, neighborhood, and financing. **(Develop your own case.)**

In stating objectives, beware of confusing the ends or goals with means to the end. For example, a worship committee in a church assigned the task of deciding what sort of worship service the church should provide might state as an objective: "Have pleasing music." However, this is not a valid objective but rather a means to a valid objective.

**Valid objectives might include:**

Maintain participation of older persons who contribute to the ministry of the church.

Attract unsaved young adults as disciples and members.

Maintain participation of present members and attract new members.

These objectives (ends) will help determine what is "pleasing music" (means to an end); but also seek to honor God.

*Though I am free and belong to no man, I make myself a slave to everyone, to win as many as possible.*—1 Cor. 9:19 (NIV)

### *Step Six*

Identify **the Boundary Conditions of the Decision**—Boundary conditions set the limits for a decision. Peter Drucker writes: "What are the objectives the decision has to reach? What are the minimum goals it has to attain? What are the conditions it has to satisfy? In science these are known as boundary conditions. A decision, to be effective, needs to satisfy the boundary conditions. It needs to be adequate to the purpose" (Drucker, The Effective Executive, p. 130). He also states that clear boundary conditions indicate what is essential and what is not, what can be compromised and what cannot.

Sometimes the boundaries are set by official, often legal, documents. A decision by a congregation, for example, ought to be within the boundaries of the church's constitution and bylaws. Or boundaries may be set by certain constraints, such as available resources. A committee in a church responsible for deciding what literature the church will use for Bible study will have boundaries set, such as funds available for literature. Acknowledging boundaries saves a person or a group a great deal of time and energy that would otherwise be spent in considering alternatives that are not possible. Of course, the boundaries should be real and actually fixed. Otherwise, the decision-making process will be limited, and creative alternatives may go unexplored.

**Obtain Opinions about Possible Options or Alternatives**—Don't start with a search for "facts" until various opinions or alternative courses of action have been spelled out. A common mistake in decision-making is to initiate a fact search before those involved have had an opportunity to think creatively and freely about possible options. The stating of alternatives or options will be informed, of course, by the boundaries and objectives, but they will not be constrained by so-called facts. The discussion on group decision-making in articles to be posted will explore in more depth the possible ways to surface these various options and alternatives.

**Gather the Facts That Relate to the Decision**—If care has been given to the previous steps, the gathering of facts will be focused and limited. On the other hand, if a person or group has not understood the nature of the decision—clearly stated objectives—and identified boundaries, countless hours may be spent gathering needless, even useless, factual material. The facts ought to relate to the actual problem and objectives within the boundaries of the decision process.

*Suppose one of you wants to build a tower. Will he not first sit down and estimate the cost to see if he has enough money to complete it?*—Luke 14:28 (NIV)

Make certain that the information gathered is actually true or factual. Do not rely on hearsay or rumor. The best way to obtain facts is to personally observe a situation.

**Abraham Lincoln** endeavored to discover for himself facts about the war effort when he was President. He spent much of his time away from his office personally visiting battlefields and government officials. Effective executives in the modern business world follow a similar strategy, sometimes referred to as **management by walking around**. However, just being out and about does not guarantee the gathering of accurate facts for decision-making. A person must develop **good listening and observing skills** in order to be effective in gathering information firsthand.

And what if it is not possible to observe "facts" firsthand? Then a person or group must **rely on reputable sources of information**. Lincoln, for example, sent trusted aides to gather factual information. Sources should be carefully checked for their reputation in providing accurate information. Just because an item is found in print or on a Web page does not insure its accuracy. Consider the source.

**Avoid over-study and over-gathering of information.** Beware of spending too much time on fact finding. Endeavor to get only what is essential. Some persons or groups are prone to continue to collect data far beyond what is needed. Why? Sometimes it is a form of procrastination: to keep gathering information is to avoid having to make a decision. Sometimes it is being too cautious: piles of information may not ensure a better decision, but it indicates that the person or group has not been lax in the effort.

### Step Seven—"Clearly State and Evaluate the Options" and
### Step Eight—"Make and Implement the Decision"

#### *Step Seven*

State **Clearly the Options or Alternatives**—By this time in the process, you should have a pretty good idea of possible options or alternatives in the decision-making process. **Write these down.** State them as clearly as possible. Don't limit yourself to what you think will be the best alternative, but list all that surface in thought, brainstorming, discussion, or whatever technique is used. Use various techniques to discover as many options as possible. Later you can determine those that are valid and those that are not. Think creatively. Ponder possibilities outside the expected. Color outside the lines. Remember that your final decision can be no better than the best alternative that you have considered.

**Evaluate the Options**—Next, eliminate the options or alternatives that are obviously unrealistic or unfeasible and identify those that seem best in light of your values, objectives, boundaries, and facts. Some of the options listed may clearly fall outside of your basic values, objectives, and boundaries and can be eliminated. The facts will help inform you of this. Of those options remaining, **carefully evaluate each one.** Various techniques can be employed to do this. Some people make a **chart of the possibilities**, listing all of the pros and cons associated with each.

Matters considered in the pros and cons should include the effect the alternative would have on a person's relation with God and others and the effect the option would have on other persons or on the organization involved.

It is reported that when making a decision, **Benjamin Franklin** would:

    —put a decision/alternative at the top of the page,
    —draw a line down the middle,
    —on one side list all the reasons **for,**

—on the other, list all the reasons **against**,

—then evaluate the merits of making the decision.

Other factors to consider are costs, resources available, time to implement, and the possible degree of resistance. In other words, endeavor to consider every possible consequence of each possible option.

**Mathematical projects and statistical analysis may be helpful** in some instances. In such cases computers are valuable tools, speeding up the process. However, keep in mind that computers are only tools and will do only what they are programmed to do. They cannot determine values or goals. That is a human process.

**Realize that there may be no perfect option.** Take time to evaluate carefully each alternative. In some cases, certain tradeoffs are involved in reaching a final decision. Disagreements are bound to arise in discussing these tradeoffs . . . even if the disagreements are within your own thought processes. This is a sign of a healthy process. In fact, **Peter Drucker advocates that a decision ought not to be made "unless there is disagreement."** (Drucker, The Effective Executive, p. 148) The desire for harmony is not bad in itself, but it can stifle creativity and result in persons' holding back valid insights because they might stir controversy.

### _Step Eight_

Make **A Tentative Decision**—If time allows, **make a tentative decision** before going public with it or acting on it. Then pray about it. See how it "feels." Sleep on it. Use your imagination to project how it will play out. Analyze the risks and uncertainties involved. Of course, you can never anticipate all of the variables and responses, but thoughtful reflection will often provide a pretty clear picture of what the decision, when carried out, will mean. Ask yourself: **"Is this decision really necessary?** Are the results anticipated in implementation worth the cost likely to be involved—in time, money, relationships, and other factors? What other decisions will this one likely lead to? Who should be involved in implementation? What plans are needed for implementation?"

Some decisions result in a long-range or action planning process. (See SkillTrack® Vol. 2, Mission-Centered Leadership.)

**Make the Decision**—Having gone through the steps and taken time for a final analysis, make the decision. Then full steam ahead! Sure, the decision might not be perfect—few if any are—but you have done your best. Avoid second-guessing your decision; however, endeavor to learn from the process of making and implementing it how to make better decisions. *A decision is not truly made until it is acted on.*

**Implement the Decision**—Decision-making does not end with making the decision—it must be acted on. Do what you decide! Implementation determines to a large degree the effectiveness of the decision. Implementation itself calls for a series of decisions:

Should implementation be delegated; if so, to whom?
Who should be informed about the decision?
In what order should persons be informed?
How should the decision be communicated?
Who should draft the decision if it is to be publicly announced?
How will the draft of the decision be released?

**Decision Actions**—To implement some decisions, you may want to call into action six stalwart soldiers:

What?
Why?
When?
Where?
How?
Who?

**Realize that there is not a single tough decision that everyone will agree with.** Resistance can be expected. People may feel threatened or hurt. Some may feel that there is a better decision—and that they can make it. Others may call for further study. A good decision maker and implementer will endeavor to anticipate the nature of resistance and opposition and the persons who most likely will react negatively. Armed with this insight, a person should prepare to implement the decision in a way to gain as much acceptance as possible.

**Develop a clear and solid rationale for the decision.** There are practical and tried ways to assist the effectiveness of implementation—not just, "God told me to do this" or "Do it because I am the one in charge." Of course, certain decisions do need to be acted on immediately by those responsible for executing them, such as soldiers on a battlefield or firemen fighting a fire, but generally persuasion is preferable to orders, commands, or coercion. Enlist key persons to help you implement the decision. One reason to include such persons in the decision-making process is so that they will be allies and not enemies in its implementation.

### Step Nine—"Assess the Effectiveness of the Decision and Process" and Step Ten—"Identify and Avoid Common Mistakes"

#### Step Nine

Assess **the Effectiveness of the Decision**—Observe the impact of the decision. Obtain feedback on its effectiveness. Is it accomplishing the objectives it was designed to achieve? If not, why not? Are certain modifications or changes called for? Of course, some decisions are irrevocable. They cannot be revised or called back. The invasion by the allied forces of Europe in World War II involved such a decision.

Once General Eisenhower made the decision to proceed, it was not reversible. However, most of the decisions we make can be modified. If the results prove that the decision was a bad one, that we have made a mistake, it is best as quickly as possible to admit it, stop the process, and start over. Mere resistance should not trigger such action, however, because generally not everyone is going to affirm the decision. Feedback that reveals success should result in continued effort to completion and celebration of the benefits of the decision.

**Analyze the Process and determine what can be learned from it**–The wise decision-maker will always debrief the decision, including its implementation. Such analysis will usually reveal ways in which the process followed may be improved or validated. Without candid evaluation, a person is doomed to repeat the same mistakes over and over again.

Don't be discouraged if the decision proves to be a faulty one. In baseball, a batter that gets a hit one-third of the times at bat is considered excellent; two-thirds of the time at bat, he fails. In making literally thousands of decisions in short periods of time, we are not going to do it right all of the time—perhaps not even most of the time. But we must continue to make decisions; to decide to not decide is to decide to let someone else make the decision! True in life and leadership! Sometimes the process is excellent, but **circumstances beyond the control of the decision-**

**maker** cause the consequences of the decision to be bad, not good. For example, a person may follow all of the decision steps in making an investment, but it results in a loss because the entire economy goes into recession—a condition over which the investor had no control. On the other hand, a flawed process can sometimes result in a positive consequence. Sometimes a tip on a stock from a questionable source pays off!

However, **in most cases the better the process of decision-making, the better the content and consequences of the decision.**

**Content and consequences of the decision:**

*An old mountaineer from West Virginia was celebrated for his wisdom. "Uncle Zed" a young man asked him, "how did you get so wise?"*

*"Weren't hard," said the old man. "I've got good judgment. Good judgment comes from experience, and experience—well, that comes from making bad judgments."*—Bethel, p. 165

### Step Ten

## HANDS ON

**Avoid the Common Mistakes in Decision-Making**—Pitfalls in the process of decision-making are numerous. Avoiding them helps make good decisions; you can improve your performance. Review the list below; then evaluate your practice of these following common mistakes in decision-making.

Use N=never; S=seldom; O=often. Where do you celebrate excellence; where do you need to improve?

_____Acting too quickly.

_____Acting too slowly.

_____Being too autocratic in group decision-making.

_____Failing to take time to clearly state the basics of the decision.

_____Focusing only on short-term results; sacrificing long-term consequences.

_____Allowing emotions to control the process.

_____Excluding emotions from the process.

_____Overlooking the biases and prejudices that shape our perception of "reality."

_____Relying too much on information from sources we know little about.

_____Ignoring feelings, intuition, "gut" reactions.

_____Seeing patterns where none exist; framing decisions on these patterns.

_____Making decisions to satisfy a current crave for variety and change.

_____Working on the wrong problem.

_____Overlooking crucial consequences of the decision.

_____Disregarding uncertainty and avoiding contingency planning.

_____Not correctly assessing your risk tolerance.

_____Being unaware of the psychological "traps": relying on first thoughts, seeing what you want to see, being too sure of yourself, etc.

_____Other

Count the total numbers of N,S,& O and place that number on the lines below. The one(s) with the highest number(s) are where you are in your process of decision-making.

How did you make out? Totals: N_____; S_____; O_____.

## Good leader and Bad leader

**From here let us look at some basic good and bad leadership traits in the quest for "Everyday Optimum Leadership."**

**Good Leaders** . . .

- Need to have a vision that is different, but still able to be accepted by the masses
- Step outside of their comfort zones to make change happen
- Take risks, make sacrifices, and sometimes pay a cost to achieve their vision
- Instill confidence in others because they themselves are confident
- Are encouragers
- Are positive
- Have the interests of others above their own
- Attract followers
- Bring new perspective to problem solving
- Are enablers
- Are an inspiration, reminder that what you say always come from deep within who you are

**Bad Leaders** . . .

- Drive wedges in between people, teams, and organizational structures
- Don't stand up for their peers or their subordinates
- Behave like children when they don't get their way
- Gossip and spread rumors
- Don't reward others for their accomplishments

- Use "techno-babble" and jargon to confuse others
- Believe they are smarter than everybody else
- Are unaware (sometimes) that most people don't respect them
- Dictate policy and doctrine almost exclusively via e-mail
- Are invisible to most of the organization
- Don't want rules, process, or procedure except for others
- Prescribe before diagnosing
- Don't solicit input from others unless it is to validate what they already believe
- Kill organizations through their arrogance and unwillingness to listen
- Are silent when they should speak / Speak when they should be silent

Bad Leaders are hurting our organizations, our governmental institutions, our local schools, churches, and neighborhoods. Bad leaders ruin opportunities for our kids, run organizations into the ground, and are culture killers. Do your part to eliminate the "cancerous" effect caused by Bad Leaders. Be an Everyday Optimum Leader by exhibiting the necessary leadership principles and ideals that inspire and motivate others. Don't be just another talking head. Be visible, don't gossip, be respectful of others, build consensus, and most of all be honest in all of your dealings.

The decisions we make in life will determine not only the very next page in our journey but when one places them all together they ultimately determine our final destination for eternity.

I enjoy movies and one really good one was, "Gladiator" with Russell Crow. In the movie there was a line he said, "What we do today will echo down throughout all eternity." How true that is, for as a leader those decisions hold a great deal of weight.

The next two chapters deal with the issue of making the wrong decisions. Maybe you have not made it yet but your maybe, what I like to call "walking on the edge." Maybe not, but in any case this is a subject that needs to be address, because in today's society it is so easy to go down the wrong path.

## CHAPTER
IV

*A decision that can bring down a leader*
*"Beware your sins will find you out"*

In the previous chapter we discussed the issues of making right decisions. This chapter deals with one of the three wrong decisions that will, if not dealt with bring down the Everyday Optimum Leader. The three are, 1) greed or the love of money 2) the desire for power and 3) sexual immorality pornography.

The issue of sexual immorality and pornography

*Part #1 . . . Step one, the path of Pornography . . .* **FANTASY**

The Internet offers both great opportunity and great peril. Back in 2002, sex-related sites became the top economic sector of the Internet, exceeding sales of both software and computers. Overall revenue from the porn industry in the United States is greater than the National Football League, National Basketball Association, and Major League Baseball combined. The dollars exchanged in adult bookstores on the corners of seedy neighborhoods pale in comparison to the reality of the online "adult super marts" in the studies and living rooms of millions of homes and offices.

**Pornography Time Statistics**

Every second—$3,075.64 is being spent on pornography . . .

Every second—28,258 Internet users are viewing pornography . . .

Every second—372 Internet users are typing adult search terms into search engines . . .

Every 39 minutes: a new pornographic video is being created in the United States . . .

**Coming into the home**

Since the advent of the Internet, the pornography industry has profited from an unprecedented proximity to the home, work and school environments. Consequently, couples, families, and individuals of *all* ages are being impacted by pornography in new and often devastating ways.

Although many parents work diligently to protect their family from sexually explicit material, research funded by Congress has shown Internet pornography to be "very intrusive." Additionally, we know that a variety of fraudulent, illegal and unethical practices are used to attract new customers and eroticize attitudes that undermine public health and safety. This profit-driven assault jeopardizes the well-being of our youth and violates the privacy of those who wish not to be exposed. Leading experts in the field of sexual addictions contend on-line sexual activity is "a hidden public health hazard exploding, in part because very few are recognizing it as such or taking it seriously."

The marital relationship is a logical point of impact to examine because it is the foundational family unit and a sexual union easily destabilized by sexual influences outside the marital contract. Moreover, research indicates the majority of Internet users are married and the majority seeking help for problematic sexual behavior online are married, heterosexual males.

The research indicates pornography consumption is associated with the following six trends, among others:

1. Increased marital distress, and risk of separation and divorce,
2. Decreased marital intimacy and sexual satisfaction,
3. Infidelity
4. Increased appetite for more graphic types of pornography and sexual activity associated with abusive, illegal or unsafe practices,
5. Devaluation of monogamy, marriage and child rearing,
6. An increasing number of people struggling with compulsive and addictive sexual behavior.

These trends reflect a cluster of symptoms that undermine the foundation upon which successful marriages and families are established.

While the marital bond may be the most vulnerable relationship to Internet pornography, children and adolescents are the most vulnerable audience.

When a child lives in a home where an adult is consuming pornography, he or she encounters the following four risks:

1. Decreased parental time and attention
2. Increased risk of encountering pornographic material
3. Increased risk of parental separation and divorce and
4. Increased risk of parental job loss and financial strain
5. When a child or adolescent is directly exposed the following effects have been documented:
6. Lasting negative or traumatic emotional responses,
7. Earlier onset of first sexual intercourse, thereby increasing the risk of STD's over the lifespan,
8. The belief that superior sexual satisfaction is attainable without having affection for one's partner, thereby reinforcing the commoditization of sex and the objectification of humans.
9. The belief that being married or having a family are unattractive prospects;
10. Increased risk for developing sexual compulsions and addictive behavior,
11. Increased risk of exposure to incorrect information about human sexuality long before a minor is able to contextualize this information in ways an adult brain could.
12. And, overestimating the prevalence of less common practices (e.g., group sex, bestiality, or sadomasochistic activity).

## The Devastating Effects

The pornography addiction takes its toll on the spouse. Many addicts have shared that the impact of cyber porn is similar if not the same as that of a real life skin-to-skin affair, in reality sin is sin in God's eye and the price is very high. Discovery often results in shocking betrayal, confusion, and shame.

It is common for a spouse faced with this crisis to believe it's her fault for not being attractive enough or sexual enough in the bedroom.

The spouse may attempt initially to increase sexual activity in order to win back the addict. Spouses sometimes agree to sexual practices, with which they are not comfortable such as having sex when they are tired, or undergoing breast enhancement surgery or liposuction. Frequently, typical codependency behaviors are utilized, such as snooping, bargaining, controlling access to the computer, and giving ultimatums. I have known some extreme cases with computer savvy spouses who would entice their addicted partner by logging into the same chat room under a false name.

Most often partners attempt to negotiate and bargain with the user to stop using the Internet. These measures end in an illusion of control. The real-life partner cannot (and should not have to) compete with the fantasy. But the porn addict loses interest in a spouse because of "ideal" relationships where there's no hassle. The experience results in emotional detachment from the marriage. The addict does not avoid sex. On the contrary, he engages in sex compulsively. However, the addict often redirects sexual interests away from the spouse and toward the computer.

The marriage enters a crisis when the partner realizes that the couple's problem-solving efforts have been unsuccessful and when the cost of remaining in the status quo becomes intolerable. I see partners who demonstrate symptoms of depression, isolation, loss of libido, and their own dysfunctional behaviors (affairs, overspending, and eating disorders) escalating, with devastating effects on their marriage, their children, and themselves.

The **spiritual** damage done by pornography use is **least visible, but the most devastating to future relationships.** In the act of sex, God paints for us a picture of our union with Christ at His return. When we mock the first institution ordained by God (marriage between a man and woman) we subvert the most sacred behavior this side of heaven.

**So where do we go from here ... let us look at four facts ...**

1.  Pornography is a growing addiction in the lives of many men. It does not have the same appeal to women. Men are more visually oriented, whereas women stress relationships. Porn has also invaded the Christian community. Men who are faithful in worship attendance also may be addicted to porn and have hidden it from their spouses for a long time. However, the effect of Porn in a marriage will be known by the wife sooner or later.

2.  Pornography is something one uses to gain a sexual turn-on, it creates an attitude of having sex with someone who is not your wife and it does not qualify as art. It creates an ego centered attitude toward sexuality rather than a responsible, loving relationship. Pornography always promises what it can't deliver. Most addictive behavior is trying to fill a need that the "fix", whether it is drugs, alcohol, gambling, or pornography, can never fill.

3.  Marriages have been lost over the addiction to pornography. Children have been abused due to the same problem. Pornography twists a man's thinking, women are viewed as sex objects, rather than a loving relationship of husband and wife.

4.  Unlike drugs which affect the body as well as the mind, <u>Pornography begins with the mind and later affects the function of the body</u>. Sexuality is dependent upon the mind first of all, and pornography distorts how one thinks about sexuality. Alaska and Nevada have the highest rape statistic in the nation and they also have the highest readership of pornography. This is ironic since Nevada has legalized prostitution.

*Part # 2 ... Step two, from fantasy to real life adultery*

In the next portion of this writing I would like to outline <u>what will happen if the issue of pornography is not dealt with</u>, and that is the person goes from a click with a fantasy online to a real live course of total destruction.

Between May and July 2003, Christianity Today International conducted mail and Internet surveys of US-based pastors and churchgoers. A total of 680 pastors and 1,972 churchgoers responded yielding a margin of error of plus or minus 4 and 2 percentage points, respectively. The survey was targeted at subscribers of the family of publications put out by the evangelical organization.

The survey showed that lay persons who committed adultery were typically in the median age of 28.5 years. Adulterous pastors were typically 32.5 years old. Today these numbers have increased substantially, showing that today this has become a problem of huge proportions. Sex outside of marriage and pornography are issues that pastors and laity alike believe are the most present problem within congregations. Furthermore, the survey showed, pastors counsel for porn addiction more frequently than any other sexual issue, and they think it is inflicting the most damage in their church. Nearly a half of pastors are counseling a parishioner on sexual issues several times a year or more.

From 1900 to 1980 divorce rose in the United States by 700%. George Barna said in 1970, that 4 out of every 10 children belong to a divorced home. Now, in 2008, it is 7 out of every 10 children that belong to a divorced home. In the church of Jesus Christ, over 60% of the marriages end in divorce. Paul said in 2 Corinthians 1:12, *"Now this is our boast: Our conscience testifies that we have conducted ourselves in the world, and especially in our relations with you, in the holiness and sincerity that are from God. We have done so not according to worldly wisdom but according to God's grace."*

The number one reason for divorce is sexual immorality. There are a lot of leaders and a lot of people and friends close to me who have fallen into adultery and immorality people that work in the market place and people that work in the church, even Senior Pastors. The following writing is about resisting sexual temptation. If you can unravel the family unit of a country, you weaken that country. The family unit is the strength and if can get it to unravel, so also goes the country. How are we doing? You have read the statistics. We are going badly. The attack is mainly on the head of the family, the man, with pornography and lust and the sexual temptation. What I want to do is show you the ease of falling into immorality and adultery.

It's like Paul says, *"We are not unaware that Satan prowls around like a roaring lion, waiting to devour."*

He (Satan) cannot take the soul of a Christian because the person who turns their life over to Jesus Christ has the Holy Spirit dwelling in them, but he can take your flesh and get you to the point where you get disqualified, distracted and **taken out.** This is one of the biggest ways that he does it. If you look in the Old Testament you will see how many great leaders and how many great men were taken out by women or immorality.

In our day and time this has almost flipped. It is just as much with the women falling into it with men. I guarantee that most of you reading this have someone close to you that has fallen into this or maybe you have fallen into this yourself. Thank God for grace.

Let us look at this so that we cannot be unaware of the devil's schemes and we can guard and protect ourselves against this. **"The Path."**

## 1. Elimination of intimacy.

Intimacy is not just sexual. Intimacy is also emotionally intimacy. It is being able to sit with your mate and communicate and be one flesh. If you get to a point in a marriage where there is an emotional vacuum, where there is the elimination of intimacy, that vacuum must be filled. If you become a butler and a maid in a marriage, there is an emotional vacuum. The intimacy in that relationship is gone. If you aren't satisfying your mate in that area, Satan has someone right around the corner that will. I promise you, he will wag that person in front of your face at the most opportune times that he can.

Proverbs 5:18 says, *"May you rejoice in the wife of your youth."* Fellows, here is a verse that you can never quote to your wife, but I can:

**1 Corinthians 7:4-6**—*"The wife's body does not belong to her alone but also to her husband. In the same way, the husband's body does not belong to him alone but also to his wife. Do not deprive each other except by mutual consent and for a time, so that you may devote yourselves to prayer. Then come together again so that Satan will not tempt because of your lack of self-control."*

If there is an elimination of that intimacy, if there is an emotional vacuum, it has to be filled and Satan will have someone right around the corner that will do that. In the move Bridges of Madison County There is this married man. He is a good provider. He is a good father. They have two kids. Meryl Streep. She is the mother she is not appreciated; she is not thanked; she is taken for granted. There develops the emotional distance between the two of them this emotional vacuum; this elimination of *intimacy* and then Satan brings in Dirty Harry, Clint Eastwood.

One day she is sitting there looking at her family, longing for some kind of acknowledgement; some kind of thanks and all you hear is the scraping of forks on the plate. The only one that cared for her was the dog. She kept saying, "It's just you and me." So even though he was a good husband and a good father, there was that elimination. There was that emotional vacuum.

**2.  Encounter.**

Now enters that person that is going to fill that emotional need. You see Clint Eastwood now comes on the scene and he laughs at her jokes, tells her she is pretty and picks flowers for her. You see him doing the little things that men do when we are courting and dating their wives. We are like hunters. We date them, court them, compliment them and do all that we can and then when we get them, we bag them and mount them on the wall like an elk. We just forget all that other stuff.

He starts doing all that stuff and you see her start to respond. The encounter could be a waitress or a banker or the church secretary. It is a filling of this emotional vacuum that she has had and this need that she has just to be appreciated. She is now getting it from him, and it is like this drug. It is a rush that she gets and she just loves it. There is flirting and there are hugs and laughing at the jokes.

Let me show you an encounter in Genesis 39. Joseph, who by the way you young studs, is about 17 at this time, which means he is probably a walking hormone. Here is Potiphar's wife, who is probably an arm piece; she is probably as fine as a mug, and here is Joseph. *"Now Joseph was well built and handsome, and after a while his master's wife took notice of Joseph and said, 'Come to bed with me!'"* There is an encounter.

Like I said, it can happen in the most unlikely places, it doesn't matter. It can be just that one person that fills that emotional vacuum. *"But he refused. 'With me in charge,' he told her, 'my master does not concern himself with anything in the house; everything he owns he has entrusted to my care. No one is greater in this house than I am.*

*My master has withheld nothing from me except you, because you are his wife. How then could I do such a wicked thing and sin against God?' And though she spoke to Joseph day after day (after day, after day, after day ...), he refused to go to bed with her or even be with her."*

So you see the encounter that can happen in the most unlikely places with the most unlikely person. One of the ladies in our church that counseled a young girl stated this girl told her, "I just wish my husband would treat me as well as he does the waitress when we go out to eat and say please and thank you and show some kind of appreciation." When you see these folks that have been married for 52 and 60 years, you just see that camaraderie; you see that emotional intimacy with conversation and how to communicate.

## 3. Enjoyment.

Now you start to build this Fantasy Island. You start picturing yourself with this person. You start thinking about how this person responds to you and how this person laughs at your jokes and how this person recognizes little things about you that your husband has either forgotten or has not mentioned. Now you want more of this little drug that you have tasted. Now you have become a junky, and you start building this great fantasy with this person. You start doing it with your thoughts. You start daydreaming. You start looking on the other side of the fence because the grass is greener over there. I heard someone say that the grass is greener on the other side of the fence because that is where you are watering with your hose.

Wherever you are watering and feeding with your thoughts is the place that's going to look like Shangri-La. You are going to think you need to be there. What has happened is your own pasture has dried up and died because you are not feeding and water it. So where you go with your thoughts will determine which pasture looks the greenest. You want to be where the pasture looks the best. You start daydreaming and thinking about it. You start thinking about what it's going to be like on the other side.

At this stage you have to make sure that you take captive every thought to make it obedient to Christ. This is where you have to sit back and say, what can I do to make my relationship with my spouse better? How can I make this side of the fence look greener? You have to start watering this side with your thoughts. You have to constantly push those impure thoughts out of your head and replace them with Godly thoughts. Like Paul says, whatever things are lovely, just, pure, and praiseworthy, you meditate on these things.

You control your thoughts. The devil doesn't make you do it. You have the choice to put into your mind what you want in there and you have the choice to push out of your mind what you don't want in there. You are thinking, "Yeah, but it's just so hard, I mean I am like Paul, the very thing I don't want to do, this I do and the very thing I do, I don't want to do. What do I do?" You take captive every thought.

You get some encouragement. You get some fellowship. You get some help. You can't just sit and dwell on these thoughts because you will build this Fantasy Island. This is what Jesus said, *"You have heard that it was said, do not commit adultery, but I tell you that anyone who looks at a woman lustfully has already committed adultery with her in his heart."* If your right eye causes you to sin, gouge it out, meaning cut off the source. Job 31:1 said, **"I made a covenant with my eyes that I may not look lustfully at a girl."** Psalm 101:3 says, **"I will set before my eyes no vile thing."** 2 Corinthians 10:5 says, **"Take every thought and make it obedient to Christ."**

For you singles, it is the same thing. It is the same thing with sexual temptation and lust just like Joseph. You don't think Joseph, at 17 years of age, didn't want to sleep with this girl? You don't think he was tempted? Do you know what it says he did? She grabbed hold of his cloak and what happened? He sprinted out of there. He would not put himself in that position. He would not stay in that situation where his brain could go there. He took off. He ran.

When you are tempted in your mind, what do you do? What did Jesus do when he was tempted by the devil three times? He used the Word of God. When you are tempted in your mind, you use the word of God. When you are temped in the flesh, you run. You get out of there. I can't tell you how many people I have counseled that say, "Well me and my girlfriend really blew it." I say, "Really, what were you doing?" They say, "Well we were alone and started kissing and things started coming off." Then they wonder why they fell.

The first nine chapters of Proverbs is talking about resisting sexual temptation; resisting that lust. Proverbs 6:20 says, **"My son, keep your father's commands and do not forsake your mother's teaching. Bind them on your heart forever; fasten them around your neck."** This means keep them sure and strong in your life. **"When you walk, they will guide you; when you sleep, they will watch over you; when you awake, they will speak to you."**

He is saying this system of truth will not let you down. **"For these commands are a lamp, this teaching is a light, and the corrections of the discipline are the way to life, keeping you from the immoral woman, from** *the smooth tongue of the wayward wife. Do not lust in your heart after her beauty or let her captivate you with her eyes.*

*For the prostitute reduces you to a loaf of bread, (she will eat you up and lick her fingers when she is done with you) and the adulteress preys upon your very life."*

So you see the elimination of intimacy, the encounter, and the enjoyment. You build this Fantasy Island with your thoughts and you start contemplating what life would be like with this person and how crappy your life is with this person and how wonderful it would be over here. It's a lie right from the pit of hell.

## 4. Expediting.

Now you start building this bridge to Fantasy Island. This is where you get off track. This is where you start playing with it like Sampson and Delilah. You know the story. He starts messing with her. His name means "light." He is the light boy to Israel. Delilah's name means "the extinguisher." She snuffs out the light and he just starts playing with it. He sees how close he can get to the fire without getting burned. What happens to Sampson at the end? Barna says he ended up blinded, binded and grinded. He got burned.

Here is what expediting means: What you do now, is start making sure that you put yourself in the path of that person that is giving you what you need and filling that emotional vacuum. If it is the secretary, you make sure you are at the water cooler or you take a break the same time she does. If it is a waitress, you find out what shift she is working and you are there. You make sure you are at the place that person is because now you need more of that drug and now you are building that bridge to Fantasy Island.

Here is where it gets very dangerous. Let's look in Proverb 7:6-9—*"At the window of my house I looked out through the lattice. I saw among the simple, I noticed among the young men, a youth who lacked judgment. He was going down the street near her corner, walking along in the direction of her house at twilight, as the day was fading."*

This young man is expediting. He is putting himself in that place where he knows he is going to have that encounter again with that person. He is going down the street near her corner, walking along the direction of her house at twilight as the day was fading. What time of day is it? It is at night and he is at the red light district.

*"As the dark of the night set in. Then out came a woman to meet him, dressed like a prostitute and with crafty intent. She is loud and defiant; her feet never stay at home."* This means there is no fear of God in this woman. She has made a covenant of marriage and it is irrelevant to her. It doesn't mean anything; there is no fear of God. *"Now in the street, now in the squares, at every corner she lurks. She took hold of him and kissed him and with a brazen face she said:"* She is tanned and looking fine. She grabs him and kisses him. She is aggressive.

Do we not have aggressive ladies today? Again, this is talking about the woman and the man; you can flip the roles here. She took a hold of him and kissed him and with brazen face she said, *"I have fellowship offerings at home; today I have fulfilled my vows."* She is saying, *"I am a Christian* and it's all in the name of Jesus. Look, I have a fish on the back of my car. This is okay. God wants you happy. Listen, you're not happy with your marriage and you're not happy with your spouse, come on.

This is okay. God gave me a word for you." I have seen more people that say God spoke to them and told them to divorce their mate. I say, "Oh, really? For what reasons?" They say, "I'm not happy." I say, "Sorry, that is not in my Bible so that isn't God speaking to you." *"I have fellowship offerings at home; today I fulfilled my vows. So I came out to meet you; I looked for you and have found you. I have covered my bed with colored linens from Egypt. I have perfumed my bed with myrrh, aloes and cinnamon."*

She is tempting him with the sense of smell. *"Come, let's drink deep of love till morning; let's enjoy ourselves with love!"* She is saying, I'm going to take care of you all night long. She paints the picture of how great and how wonderful this experience is going to be. *"My husband is not at home; he has gone on a long journey. He took his purse filled with money and will not be home till full moon."*

She is saying, we won't get caught, nobody will know. *"With persuasive words she led him astray; she seduced him with her smooth talk. All at once he followed her like an ox going to the slaughter, like a deer stepping into a noose, till an arrow pierces his liver, like a bird darting into a snare, little knowing it will cost him his life."*

If you get shot in the liver, you pretty much die a slow, bleeding out death. That is what Solomon is saying here. If you start messing around like this, it ends badly. *"Now then, my son, listen to me; pay attention to what I say. Do not let your heart turn to her ways or stray into her paths. Many are the victims she has brought down; her slain are a mighty throng. Her house is a highway to the grave (hell), leading down to the champers of death."* How serious do you think Solomon is here?

## 5. Expression.

Now you have crossed over the bridge. Now you unload your heart. It is like verbal tennis. There are phone calls and emails that might go like this: "Man, I sure like spending time with you." "Me too." "Man, it's just so much better when I'm with you than it is with my husband." "Yeah, me too. My wife doesn't make me feel this way." "Yeah, neither does my husband." And you go back and forth with his verbal tennis and now you are expressing yourself. Now you have done everything except for doing the act. When you get to this expression point and start unloading your heart and you get that affirmation on the other side, it is over.

Proverbs 4:24 *"Put away perversity from your mouth; keep corrupt talk far from your lips."* Life and death are in the power of the tongue. In Proverbs 6:27 Solomon says, *"Can a man scoop fire into his lap without his clothes being burned."*

If you start playing in this area, you are going to get burned. You argue, "Yeah, but they make me feel so good. They make me feel alive. They make me feel like my husband never made me feel. They make me feel like my wife never made me feel." You made a covenant with God almighty and God does not take lightly vows that are broken.

Ephesians 4:29 says, ***"Do not let any unwholesome talk come out of your mouths, but only what is helpful for building others up according to their needs, that it may benefit those who listen."***

Okay, now you have elimination of intimacy, then the encounter, then you have that enjoyment and become a junky, then you expedite and put yourself in that position, then you express it with your heart. Again singles, it's the same thing. You stay away from this because it is the same pattern whether you are single or married.

## 6. Experience.

At this point, you go right to the experience. It is done. After you have expressed your heart, it is just a matter of getting alone or finding someplace and you go for the experience. Here is the danger and this is what I tell folks: You have to look past the pleasure to the pain. Look to your Savior, Lord Jesus Christ for number one. Then you look to people closest associated with you such as family, children, and colleagues. You have to look past the pleasure to the pain.

Hebrews 11: 25—Moses, ***"He chose to be mistreated along with the people of God rather than to enjoy the pleasures of sin for a short time. He regarded disgrace for the sake of Christ as of greater value than the treasures of Egypt."*** This was because he was looking ahead to his reward.

The Everyday Optimum Leader needs to look past the pleasure to the pain because sin is good for a season and then Satan runs off laughing **when you fall**.

## The heart of the matter

So what is at the heart of this matter, it is simple . . .

*"For all that is in the world, the lust of the flesh and the lust of the eyes and the pride of life, is not of the Father but is of the world"*
*(1 John 2:15).*

Lust is defined as the disordered or unrestrained seeking of sexual/genital pleasure. The lustful person pursues excessively the good of sex which is intended for the good of the human race. A lustful person will do whatever is necessary to gain disordered pleasure. Lust invites us to pursue sexual pleasure for its own sake without weighing the consequences, and to focus so much on our own satisfaction that other moral instincts are pushed aside. Lust is an offence against ourselves, against other persons, and against society. Lust is a capital vice because it leads to other vices/sins—blindness of mind, perversion of heart, rashness, inconstancy, inordinate self-love, fornication, masturbation, pornography, etc. The lustful person becomes blind to all else as he seeks to gratify his base desires.

Since we are by nature sexual beings endowed with sexual desires, some regulation of our sexual appetite is required (2 Tim. 2:22, Titus 2:6). The virtue of **chastity** moderates and regulates the sexual appetite or genital pleasure according to the principles of right reason and the law of God. Chastity is not simply a restrictive virtue. It consists in the right attitude towards sex. It also enables us to reach self-control or self-mastery and it liberates us from the bondage of self-centered, aggressive, manipulative sexual activity. Continence is a virtue of the will by which the Everyday Optimum Leader checks their strong impulses to make extremely wrong decisions.

## Examples from the scripture

In Genesis 39:7-21, we read the account of Potiphar's wife trying to seduce Joseph into adultery. Joseph's immediate instinct was to flee temptation. Joseph was chaste in his relations with women and remained faithful to God's law. David committed adultery (2 Samuel 11) and Solomon had many wives (1 Kings 11). Both were spiritually weakened and were punished by God for their unchaste living.

*"Therefore honor God with your body" (1 Cor. 6:20).*

The decision for the Everyday Optimum Leader to, "honor God with their body," starts in their mind. By doing so they will be useful to God and be in a powerful position to affect many.

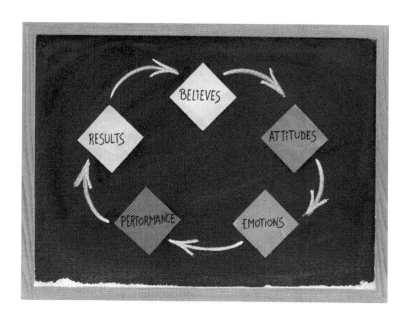

# CHAPTER
## V

*Walking on the edge of a wrong decision*

## "Walking on the edge of a wrong decision"

*"Blessed is the man who **walks** not in the counsel of the ungodly, Nor **stands** in the path of sinners, Nor **sits** in the seat of the scornful; But his delight is in the law of the Lord and His law he mediates day and night.*

*He shall be like a tree planted by the rivers of water, that <u>brings forth its fruit in its season,</u> whose leaf also <u>shall not wither</u>; and whatever he does <u>shall prosper.</u>"—Psalms 1: 1-3*

There is a progression to this venture down the road of walking on the edge of a wrong decision or residing in the land of questionable ethics . . .

## Ethical norms . . . Reason based system:

Here the basis idea is that ethical norms are generated from and discernible by reason.

In other words, you and I know better in our hearts, but we don't always do right.

Romans 1:18-21 & 2: 14-16

[18] *The wrath of God is being revealed from heaven against all the godlessness and wickedness of people, who suppress the truth by their wickedness,* [19] *since what may be known about God is plain to them, because God has made it plain to them.* [20] *For since the creation of the world God's invisible qualities—his eternal power and divine nature—have been clearly seen, being understood from what has been made, so that people are without excuse.* [21] *For although they knew God, they neither glorified him as God nor gave thanks to him, but their thinking became futile and their foolish hearts were darkened.*

[14] *(Indeed, when Gentiles, who do not have the law, do by nature things required by the law, they are a law for themselves, even though they do not have the law.* [15] *They show that the requirements of the law are written on their hearts, their consciences also bearing witness, and their thoughts sometimes accusing them and*

*at other times even defending them.)* [16] *This will take place on the day when God judges people's secrets through Jesus Christ, as my gospel declares.*

**BIBLICAL ETHICS**—living righteously—doing what is good and refraining from what is evil—in accordance with the will of God. The term refers not to human theories or opinions about what is right and wrong but to God's revealed truth about these matters.

Questions of human conduct prevail throughout the Bible. God's revelation through His written Word narrates the story of ethical failure on the part of human beings, God's redeeming grace, and the ethical renewal of His people. God's people are called to holiness because they are God's people: "You shall therefore be holy, for I am holy" (Lev. 11:45). The New Testament counterpart to this principle is found in Matthew 5:48: "Therefore you shall be perfect, just as your Father in heaven is perfect." (Perfect here means mature).

**The temptation to walk on that edge:**

*"You cannot play with the animal in you without becoming wholly animal, play with falsehood without forfeiting your right to truth, play with cruelty without losing your sensitivity of mind. He who wants to keep his garden tidy does not reserve a spot for weeds."—Author Unknown*

We are tempted to get close to that edge . . .

The Lord does not condemn us for being tempted. In fact, He is sympathetic and He knows the temptation that we face.

The Bible tells us, *"For we do not have a High Priest who cannot sympathize with our weaknesses, but was in all points tempted as we are, yet without sin."—Hebrews 4:15*

It is equally important to read the verse right after . . ." *Let us therefore come boldly to the throne of grace, that we may obtain mercy and find grace to help in* **time of need**.*"—Hebrews 4:16*

Every leader, every person on earth needs His grace.

**There are three things that lead us to walk on this edge:**

We are tempted by Satan, our flesh, and the world.

*"Let no one say when he is tempted, 'I am tempted by God'; for God cannot be tempted by evil, nor does He Himself tempt anyone. But each one is tempted when he is **drawn away** by **his own desires** and enticed."*—James 1:13-14

*I want . . . I want . . . I want . . . **This edge leads to a slippery slope** . . .*

The main source of temptation is our own fleshly nature. Jesus Himself said that we will be tempted, and the Apostle Paul tells us, **1)** *".**Knowing** this, that our old man was crucified with Him, that the body of sin might be done away with, that we should no longer be slaves of sin. For he who has died has been freed from sin . . . likewise you also, **2) to reckon** yourselves to be dead indeed to sin, but alive to God in Christ Jesus our Lord.*

*Therefore do not let sin reign in your mortal body, that you should obey it in its lust . . . for sin shall not **3) have dominion** over you, for you are not under law but under grace."*—Romans 6:6-7, 11-12, 14.

**Walking on the edge leads to lying on the edge:**

In the world of business and life itself it is becoming so easy to lie. It is estimated that as many as 44% of all college students lie (cheat) to pass their exams.

Bob Moorhead, author of Counsel Yourself and Others from the Bible states that there are seven reasons why people lie . . .

1. To get their own way
2. Feelings of inferiority
3. To be accepted by others
4. To avoid consequences

5. To maintain an image they want to project to others
6. For material gain
7. They have become duplicitous

For some in business this seems to be, "the way they do business."

*"These six things the Lords hates, yes, seven are an abomination to Him: A proud look a lying tongue, hands that shed innocent blood, a heart that devises wicked plans, feet that are swift in running to evil, a false witness who speaks lies, and one who sows discord among brethren."*

*Proverbs 6:16-19*

To make that deal is it OK to just edge around the real truth?

If you knew it would cost you to tell the truth . . . would you do it?

"It's just a little white lie," or, "I didn't lie, I just didn't say anything."

To lie is to make a person believe what is not true; mislead; act of fraud. When we lie we are misleading people, committing fraud against them, and ultimately harming them and ourselves.

The Bible tells us to be people of our word. The most loving, Christ-like character trait we can hold is to be a person of integrity—a person who is honest and trustworthy.

**Walking on the edge for the sake of greed:**

*"Do not overwork to be rich; because of your own understanding, cease! Will you set your eyes on that which is not? For riches certainly make themselves wings; they fly away like an eagle toward heaven."—Proverbs 23:4-5*

At the root of this problem is greed. Greed is an excessive desire for money and material possessions. A greedy person is never satisfied with what they have, yet the Bible tells us to be content with what God has given us.

*"Now godliness with contentment is great gain."—1 Timothy 6:6*

This greed thing comes from our hearts. It is an attitude and a value system. There are some very greedy people who are millionaires, and there are some very greedy people who live on welfare. It has been said that, "one of the weaknesses of our age is our apparent inability to distinguish our **needs** from our **greeds**."

**What does this walk with greed cause us to do?**

It can lead to evil actions! The love of money is the root of all evil. Because of greed, people lie in business to close that deal, some will become drug sellers, thieves, and on and one it can go. It can cause a person to take advantage of others! A greedy person in business is a selfish person. They step on people and use them to reach the top. Their greed often drives them to oppress the poor, something the Bible strongly condemns.

*"He who oppresses the poor reproaches his Maker, but he who honors Him has mercy on the needy."– Proverbs 14:31*

**The walk of an ethical and moral person:**

Because of the present moral crisis, one does not have to be a prophet to be able to predict that Western civilization can only go in one or two directions.

It can either return to the Judeo-Christian ethic which made the West the great civilization it was, or it can move toward the tyranny of totalitarianism.

Since we have already departed from our roots and are moving toward the latter, it has been said, "The only thing that saves us while we are in this transition is fear."

What prevents a person today from committing a crime? Not a strong sense of right or wrong, but a fear of getting caught!

## Walking in alignment with God.

God's Character . . .

The foundation of Christian ethics in business and in life in general is not rules but the changeless character of God. Scripture describes God as being the creator of all things, perfect, preceding and superseding all things. It also tells how we as human beings were originally created to emulate God. As a Christian we operate on the notion that ethics (the study of human character) logically follows theology (the study of God's character).

## A walk that aligns with God's character:

Question, what is the character of God? As we look at the Bible we see three divine characteristics that have direct bearing on ethical decision-making.

1. God is holy
2. God is just
3. God is loving

Christian ethics requires all three characteristics to be taken into account when decisions are made.

Holiness, when un-tethered from justice and love, drifts into hypercritical legalism. Justice that loses its anchor in holiness and love produces harsh outcomes. Love when it is orphaned lacks an adequate moral compass. Each contains a vital ethical ingredient. Christian ethics does not involve "either/or" analysis as if we could chose between holiness, justice and love—but rather a synthesis in which all three conditions must be met before an action can be considered moral.

Regarding Holiness:

*"Make every effort to be holy; without holiness no one will see the Lord."*— *Hebrews 12:14*

Martin Luther said—"You cannot stop the birds from flying over your head, but you can keep them from building a nest in your hair."

Regarding Justice:

Augustine said—"A society without justice is no better than a band of thieves."

Regarding Love:

*"And now abide faith, hope, love, these three; but the greatest of these is love."*– 1 Corinthians 13:13

**Walking in God's character:**

It is too easy for all of us to gravitate toward moral errors . . .

- Idolize business success
- Set lower ethical standards in the marketplace
- Exploit employees
- Abuse the environment

We all fall far short of the holiness—justice—love standard. Don't be overly discouraged by this ethical deficit, we should humbly accept God's offer of grace. Through the death of his Son there is forgiveness; through his Holy Spirit there is hope of moral improvement. This is why even our ethical failings can have a silver lining. Recognizing our imperfections, we are drawn to the grace of God which in turn leads us to assess ourselves modestly and to treat others the way God treats us. These elements keep the Everyday Optimum Leader on the right path in life, business and in the church.

## Moral Failure of the leader

### 1. Defining Moral Failure by Sexual Indiscretion:

Whenever some Christian leader is sat down, the term "moral failure" is generally volleyed around. Yesterday I asked a few people, what is moral failure and the answers I got all were "usually some sort of sexual indiscretion." I believe that is part of the problem. Perhaps they've been led to believe that other moral failings don't matter as long as it's not sex, therefore they allow the small foxes to go unchecked meanwhile those same "small indiscretions" are steadily snowballing into the avalanche that eventually derails them and ultimately embarrasses them publicly.

And the public embarrassment is the part that bothers me the most because it shows that people don't necessarily have any private accountability. They are only concerned if they are "caught or found out." It's as if God is not real to them. As if when they were in the booth, in the back, in the corner and in the dark that the Holy Spirit did not follow them there. Perhaps the standard should be set higher than sex for a leader in particular. This is why I commend a man by the name of Kirk Franklin years ago for getting help for his pornography addiction. He did not necessarily have to come out and tell us about it. He was only obligated to tell his wife, but he realized that a struggle between he and his computer screen was too an issue.

There are all sorts of areas of compromise that are out there beyond sex, and those issues are just as much an issue as sex. I guess I am trying to say, by the time you've reached the act of sexual expression outside of the covenant marriage you've already passed a few other stop signs of compromise to get there that went unchecked and should have been dealt with.

### 2. Setting up Safe Guards:

I'll admit I was real disappointed when I read an article by Shaun King (pastor of Courageous Church) about **"Drastic Measures to Avoid Moral Failure."** I was proud of Shaun, but disappointed with the readers who commented that he was over-reacting. I feel like Shaun was doing the right thing. The Bible tells us not to put any confidence in the flesh. One scripture that I always revert back to is 1 Corinthians 10:12 which says, *"Let him who thinks he stands, take heed lest he fall"* meaning even if you think you've got it together, be careful because resting on your past ability to fight temptations could catch you slipping. That same verse in the Message translation reads like this

*"Don't be so naive and self confident. You are not exempt. You could fall flat on your face as easily as anyone else. Forget about self-confidence, it's useless. Cultivate God-confidence"*

Safeguards are important for leaders. It is also important for those around those leaders to respect the safeguards that they have in place. When leaders signed up to be a leader that meant that the standard was raised for them and are held to the strictest standards. James 3:1 says, *"My brethren, let not many of you become teachers, knowing that we shall receive a stricter judgment."* However, non-leaders, the same thing you expect from your leader you should carry out in your own life because you answer to the same God.

3. **Birds of a Feather** ... :

You've heard the saying that birds of a feather flock together. That's a biblical concept. Who you hang around generally can shape your worldview and "moral vision." It doesn't surprise me that Da T.R.U.T.H was the third artist from Cross Movement Records to be dismissed for infidelity. They failed each other as accountability partners; instead they may have been covering for one another. Who knows? 1 Corinthians 15:33 says *"Do not be deceived: 'Evil company corrupts good habits.'"* In other words, bad company corrupts good morals.

4. **Learn Vicariously:**

All that being said. Do I believe that Da T.R.U.T.H. can recover? Of course. Should we pray for him to get better and restored? Absolutely.

Does the Bible tell us how to handle situations like that? Yes and the Bible is clear on doing it in love. But here is the lesson for leaders. Learn vicariously through the mistake of others. If you've been in some type of compromise, you've been under grace and mercy. Turn around. Be a person of integrity.

—The area in your life you fail to deal with, could be responsible for your downfall

—The area of character you refuse to develop is the open door you fail to close to the devil.

Definition of moral failure: an event that does not accomplish the intended purpose of conforming to the standards, behavior and character based on the principles of right and wrong.

## What can we learn from fallen Christian Leadership?

When I first heard the news that Ted Haggard, the former senior pastor of New Life Church in Colorado Springs, Colorado, had resigned amidst accusations of sexual misconduct and for purchasing illegal drugs, my heart was grieved. I was so upset I didn't dare speak or even write about it. As the accusations proved to be true, I continued to grieve. I grieved for Ted, his family and his congregation of over 14,000. I grieved for the body of Christ, and for myself. I knew this scandal would affect the entire Christian community. You see, Ted Haggard was also the president of the National Association of Evangelicals. He was well-known and often quoted by the media. Christians everywhere were hard hit with the news. Fragile Christians would be devastated and certainly skeptics would turn away from Christianity.

## Whenever a high-profile Christian leader falls or fails, the effects are far-reaching.

For a while I felt anger at Ted for not getting help sooner. I was angry at Satan for devouring another Christian testimony. I felt sadness for the pain this scandal would cause Ted's family and his large sphere of influence. I felt sadness for the gays, prostitutes, and drug abusers focused on by this scandal. I felt embarrassment for the name of Christ and for his church. This would be one more opportunity for mocking Christians, for pointing out the hypocrisy within the church. And then I felt ashamed for judging my brother, for overlooking my own hidden sin, my own failures and short comings.

**Something like this can happen to any one of us if we do not remain vigilant in our walk with Christ.**

When anger and shame subsided I felt some comfort too. For I know when sin is kept hidden in darkness, it flourishes, entangling and blinding as it grows in strength. But once exposed, once confessed and ready to be dealt with, sin loses its grip, and a prisoner goes free.

**Psalm 32:3-5**

*When I kept silent, my bones wasted away through my groaning all day long. For day and night your hand was heavy upon me; my strength was sapped as in the heat of summer. Then I acknowledged my sin to you and did not cover up my iniquity. I said, "I will confess my transgressions to the LORD"—and you forgave the guilt of my sin. (NIV)*

I asked God to help me learn from this terrible tragedy in Ted Haggard's life—to keep me from ever experiencing a crushing fall. During my time of contemplation, I was inspired to write this practical reflection of what we as believers can learn from fallen Christian leaders.

**First, we can learn to respond with love, grace and forgiveness.**
But how does that look in the practical sense?

**1.  Pray for Fallen Leaders**

We all have hidden sin, we all fall short. We all are capable of failing. Leaders make enticing targets for the devil's schemes because the greater the leader's influence, the greater the fall. The overwhelming consequences of the fall create greater destructive power for the enemy. So our leaders need our prayers.

When a Christian leader falls, pray that God will wholly restore, heal and rebuild the leader, their family and every person affected by the fall. Pray that through the devastation, God's purpose will be completely accomplished, that God will receive greater glory in the end, and that God's people will be strengthened.

## 2. Extend Forgiveness to Fallen Leaders

A leader's sin is no worse than my own. The blood of Christ covers and cleanses it all.

### Romans 3:23
*For everyone has sinned; we all fall short of God's glorious standard.* (NLT)

### 1 John 1:9
*If we confess our sins, he is faithful and just and will forgive us our sins and purify us from all unrighteousness.* (NIV)

## 3. Guard Yourself against Judging Fallen Leaders

Be careful not to judge, lest you be judged also.

### Matthew 7:1-2
*Do not judge, or you too will be judged. For in the same way you judge others, you will be judged . . .* (NIV)

## 4. Extend Grace to Fallen Leaders

The Bible says that love covers sins and offenses (Proverbs 10:12; Proverbs 17:9; 1 Peter 4:8). Love and grace will encourage you to keep quiet instead of speculating about the circumstances and gossiping about the fallen brother or sister. Imagine yourself in the situation and think about the leader as you would want others considering you in the same position. You will prevent the devil from wreaking further havoc as a result of the sin, if you simply keep quiet and cover that person with love and grace.

**Proverbs 10:19**

*When words are many, sin is not absent, but he who holds his tongue is wise.* (NIV)

**What Else Can We Learn from Fallen Christian Leaders?**

- **Leaders should not be placed on pedestals.**

Leaders should not live on pedestals, either of their own making or built by their followers. Leaders are men and women too, made of flesh and blood. They are vulnerable in every way you and I are. When you place a leader on a pedestal, you can be sure that someday, somehow they will disappoint you. Whether leading or following each of us must come to God in humility and dependence on a daily basis. If we begin to think we are above this, we will drift from God. We will open ourselves up to sin and pride.

**Proverbs 16:18**

*Pride goes before destruction, and haughtiness before a fall.* (NLT)

So, don't place yourself, or your leaders on a pedestal.

- **Sin that destroys a leader's reputation does not happen overnight.**

Sin begins with a thought or an innocent look. When we dwell on the thought or we revisit with a second glance, we invite sin to grow. Little by little we go deeper and deeper until we are so entangled in sin we don't even want to be freed. I have no doubt this is how a leader like Ted Haggard eventually found himself caught in sin.

## James 1:14-15

*Temptation comes from our own desires, which entice us and drag us away. These desires give birth to sinful actions. And when sin is allowed to grow, it gives birth to death.* (NLT)

So, don't let sin entice you. Flee from the first sign of temptation.

- **A leader's sin does not offer a license for you to sin.**

Don't let someone else's sin encourage you to continue in your own sin. Let the terrible consequences they are suffering cause you to confess your sin and get help now, before your situation gets any worse. Sin is not something to play around with. If your heart is truly set to follow God, he will do what is necessary to expose your sin.

## Numbers 32:23

*. . . be sure your sin will find you out.* (NASB)

- **Having sin exposed is the best thing for the leader.**

Although the horrible aftermath of the fallen leader's scandal may seem like the worst possible circumstance with no positive outcome, don't despair. Remember God is still in control. Most likely he is allowing the sin to be exposed so that repentance and restoration can come into the person's life. What seems like a victory for the devil may actually be God's hand of mercy, saving a sinner from further destruction.

## Romans 8:28

*And we know that all things work together for good to them that love God, to them who are the called according to his purpose.* (KJV)

It's important to keep in mind that all of God's chosen leaders in the Bible, the great ones and the not-so-well-known ones, were imperfect men and women. Moses and David committed murder—Moses, before God called him, and David, after God called him into service. Jacob was a cheater, Solomon and Samson had problems with women. God used prostitutes and thieves and every kind of sinner imaginable to prove that man's fallen condition is not what matters in God's eyes. It is God's greatness—his power to forgive and restore—that should make us bow down in worship and wonder. We should always be in awe of his importance and his desire to use someone like you, someone like me. In spite of our fallen condition, God sees us as valuable—each and every one of us.

## Rescuing the fallen leader, in the church and the marketplace

If we knew the actual numbers, we would not like them.

Every year in nearly every denomination, men or women who are in some role of church leadership commit immorality that costs them their positions and puts their families in jeopardy. Some commit adultery. Others are caught with pornography on their computers. Pick the sin—start with the A's and go to the Z's—and it's likely that someone trusted as a leader in the kingdom of God has done it and finally been exposed. The same goes for the Christian in the marketplace.

Though we acknowledge that all of us are human, we expect one who is mature enough to serve in leadership is also one that is honest enough with self and God to live a life of holiness. We tend to see their sins as worse than the sins of John Q. Member who sporadically attends and has little involvement with the church. Therefore, when we discover the immorality of one of our leaders, whether on a national or local scale, we passionately proclaim our deep care for their souls and cry with them as they resign their roles, all the while hoping against hope that they pack up and move away as quickly as possible.

## That is understandable

The hurt, the sense of loss, and the feelings of being betrayed by a trusted person are powerful. Pretending the offense does not threaten the health of the church and passionately pleading that good Christians forgive and allow a fallen leader to continue in her role uninterrupted is not a valid course of action (ask the churches who tried that method!). There are repercussions in the church, weaker Christians to think of, sin to deal with, and usually a scrambling to reorganize to cover the gap created by the fallen leader. In the marketplace as a Christian business person the damage brought to the company, the destroyed trust that could and many times does reach all the way to the bottom line, translation loose of revenue because you lose some of your Christian clients.

However, in dealing with the sin and its consequences, this question should also be preeminent. Would it be good for the kingdom at large if we could rescue fallen leaders rather than making refuse of them?

We know that people with unloving hearts sometimes do good things, but that their good deeds do not wonderfully transform them into good, loving people (Matthew 7:22, 23). We also know that good, loving people sometimes do bad things (Romans 3:10, 23). Does an act, or an era of failing, definitely indicate that a person with a good heart has become bad or evil? Of course not. God redeemed King David after his adultery and used him in His work. He redeemed betrayal by Peter and made him a great apostle. He can and does do the same today with those who have lost their influence or positions through their own sin. These men and women can and should be restored, but with wisdom and circumspection.

## Remove Responsibility

To restore a fallen leader, there must first be a period of healing and recovery. Now one would say, what just a minute how can a CEO or manager in a company remove him/herself? The answer is the need to go before their board, state what has happened, place a trusted associate in their position and explain that they need time to let God speak to them, search their heart, repent and see what God will do. This action, though it may seem drastic by nature it will be a powerful tool to restore the leader first to the leader and to the company as a whole. This action of "doing the right thing," clears the air, sets a standard for integrity and opens a positive door to healing and a good future.

Some of the following basic issues regarding the restoration of leadership in a church setting can and should apply to the fallen leader in the marketplace. Regarding the church, a lead minister of a rather large church argued that because he publicly repented when his affair was exposed, he should not be required to step down from his leadership position. An associate pastor left the church that dismissed him for immorality, taking about 300 people with him, and started a new church immediately. A youth minister claimed that he was sorry for his sexual liaison with an underage teen in his group, and, therefore, if the parents in his congregation were truly Christian, they would not treat him so coldly.

Galatians 6:7-8 teaches that there are consequences for our actions, both good and bad. For a leader to stumble badly and then to go on as if there has not been a great breach in her spirituality is to ignore that truth. Maturity and concern for the kingdom should lead her to understand that there must be a sabbatical from leadership during which she can heal spiritually, emotionally, and mentally. There should also be time for the congregation or organization to heal.

From the examples of some of well-known Christians who fell into immorality and refused to step down, we learned that their refusal may indicate a lack of contrition or acceptance of responsibility for their actions. During the time that the leader is no longer leading, the right resources must be made available for him and his family for spiritual scrutiny, marital restoration, and ministry renovation.

## Spiritual Scrutiny

Those who teach have great responsibility, whether they choose to remember that or not (James 3:1). Those who lead must care for and nurture the church of God (Acts 20:28). When one who leads others to righteousness fails to live righteously, there should be an analysis of what he is missing spiritually, and what areas of his life and calling need growth. To think that a spiritual leader simply "made a mistake" that can be forgotten with an apology is to misunderstand the process through which a person goes to move from spiritual leadership to moral failure.

Others in the kingdom may cast a fallen leader aside and expect him or her to figure these things out. The better course of action is for wise, mature Christians to step in and guide the process, either formally or informally (though formally is usually better). Someone should care enough to rescue those who can be rescued.

Those who are helped often are raised up by God again to be leaders in the kingdom.

God wins.

Satan loses.

## Marital Restoration

Typically a moral failure does more than cost a leader his position in the kingdom and marketplace. Nearly always there are strained marriages and damaged families. This is particularly true if the immorality involved another person or some type of sexual sin.

If you are able to work with these leaders and help them rescue their marriages, we serve God in thwarting Satan's schemes. If the marriage fails, the likelihood of restoring the fallen leader to a position of leadership again diminishes. He may find himself back in step spiritually and again used by God, but some opportunities in the kingdom may well be withheld because of their failed marriage. Additionally, saving their marriages may well be the catalyst for saving their children's futures so that they do not grow up to be bitter either by what their parent has done or by how the church or other leadership in the marketplace reacted.

When churches and other leadership in the marketplace are not focused altogether on their own pain, they think about how important this is. If every church made it a priority not only to remove the leader from leadership responsibility until healing takes place, but also to aid her spiritual life and rescue her marriage, we would have a cadre of restored leaders who not only have spiritual wellness, but who understand how to rescue sinners in a way that many Christians never will. Rather than decrying the loss of leaders in the business world and the decline of churches, the kingdom could rejoice in salvaging sinners—even those who should have known better—and taking the gospel to the world in a way that proclaims Christ's love to those who are NOT perfect.

# CHAPTER
## VI

*Optimum Leadership Instruments*
## HANDS ON

## Leadership Instruments

### Question ... what are they?

The following are qualitative and quantitative instruments to be used as a guide to measure your Everyday Optimum Leadership inward traits and styles.

Multifactor Leadership Questionnaire (MLQ)

This questionnaire provides a description of your leadership style. Twenty-one descriptive statements are listed below. Judge how frequently each statement fits you. The word others may mean your followers, clients, or group members.

Key: 0=not at all, 1=Once in a while, 2=Sometimes, 3=Fairly often, 4=Frequently is not always.

1.  I make others feel good to be around me.                          1 2 3 4
2.  I express with a few simple words what we could
    and should do.                                                     1 2 3 4
3.  I enable others to think about old problems in new ways.          1 2 3 4
4.  I help others develop themselves.                                  1 2 3 4
5.  I tell others what to do if they want to be rewarded
    for their work.                                                    1 2 3 4
6.  I am satisfied when others meet agreed-upon standards.            1 2 3 4
7.  I am content to let others continue working
    in the same way as always.                                        1 2 3 4
8.  Others have complete faith in me.                                  1 2 3 4
9.  I provide appealing images about what we can do.                  1 2 3 4
10. I provide others with new ways of looking
    at puzzling things.                                                1 2 3 4
11. I let others know how I think they are doing.                     1 2 3 4
12. I provide recognition / rewards when others
    reach their goals.                                                 1 2 3 4

13. As long as things are working, I do not try
 to change anything.                                      1 2 3 4
14. Whatever others want to do is OK with me.              1 2 3 4
15. Others are proud to be associated with me.             1 2 3 4
16. I help others find meaning in their work.              1 2 3 4
17. I get others to rethink ideas that they had never
 questioned before.                                        1 2 3 4
18. I give personal attention to others who seem rejected.  1 2 3 4
19. I call attention to what others can get for what
 they accomplish.                                          1 2 3 4
20. I tell others the standards they have to know
 to carry out their work.                                  1 2 3 4
21. I ask no more of others than what is absolutely essential.  1 2 3 4

Scoring

The MLQ-6S measures your leadership on seven factors related to transformational leadership. Your score for each factor is determined by summing three specified items on the questionnaire.

For example, to determine your score for Factor 1, idealized influence, sum your responses for items 1, 8, and 15. Complete this procedure for all seven factors.

Idealized influence (items 1,8,and 15)               Factor 1=
Inspirational motivation (items 2,9, and 16)         Factor 2=
Intellectual stimulation (items 3,10, and 17)        Factor 3=
Individualized consideration (items 4,11, and 18)    Factor 4=
Contingent reward (items 5,12, and 19)               Factor 5=
Management-by-exception (items 6,13, and 20)         Factor 6=
Laissez-faire Leadership (items 7,14, and 21)        Factor 7=

Score range: High = 9-12, Moderate = 5-8, Low = 0-4

Scoring Interpretation

Factor 1. Idealized influence indicates whether you hold subordinates' trust, maintain their faith and respect, show dedication to them, appeal to their hopes and dreams, and act as their role model.

Factor 2. Inspirational motivation measures the degree to which you provide a vision, use appropriate symbols and images to help others focus on their work, and try to make others feel their work is significant.

Factor 3. Intellectual stimulation shows the degree to which you encourage others to be creative in looking at old problems in new ways, create an environment that is tolerant of seemingly extreme positions, and nurture people to question their own values and beliefs and those of the organization.

Factor 4. Individualized consideration indicates the degree to which you show interest in others' well being, assign projects individually, and pay attention to those who seem less involved in the group.

Factor 5. Contingent reward shows the degree to which you tell others what to do in order to be rewarded, emphasize what you expect from them, and recognize their accomplishments.

Factor 6. Management-by-exception assesses whether you tell others the job requirements, are content with standard performance, and are a believer in "if it isn't broke, don't fix it."

Factor 7. Laissez-faire measures whether you require little of others, are content to let things ride, and let others do their own thing.

## Style Questionnaire

Read each item carefully and think about how often you engage in the described behavior. Indicate your response to each item by circling one of the five numbers to the right of each item.

Key: 1=never 2=Seldom 3=Occasionally 4=Often 5=Always

| | | |
|---|---|---|
| 1. | Tells group members what they are supposed to do | 1 2 3 4 5 |
| 2. | Acts friendly with members of the group | 1 2 3 4 5 |
| 3. | Sets standards of performance for group members | 1 2 3 4 5 |
| 4. | Helps others feel comfortable in the group | 1 2 3 4 5 |
| 5. | Makes suggestions about how to solve problems | 1 2 3 4 5 |
| 6. | Responds favorably to suggestions made by others | 1 2 3 4 5 |
| 7. | Makes his/her perspective clear to others | 1 2 3 4 5 |
| 8. | Treats others fairly | 1 2 3 4 5 |
| 9. | Develops a plan of action for the group | 1 2 3 4 5 |
| 10. | Behaves in a predictable manner toward group members | 1 2 3 4 5 |
| 11. | Defines roles responsibilities for each group member | 1 2 3 4 5 |
| 12. | Communicates actively with group members | 1 2 3 4 5 |
| 13. | Clarifies his/her own role within the group | 1 2 3 4 5 |
| 14. | Shows concern for the personal well-being of others | 1 2 3 4 5 |

15. Provides a plan for how the work is to be done     1 2 3 4 5

16. Shows flexibility in making decisions     1 2 3 4 5

17. Provides criteria for what is expected of the group     1 2 3 4 5

18. Discloses thoughts and feelings to group members     1 2 3 4 5

19. Encourages group members to do quality work     1 2 3 4 5

20. Helps group members get along     1 2 3 4 5

## Scoring

The style questionnaire is designed to measure two major types of leadership behavior: task and relationship. Score the questionnaire by doing the following. First, sum the responses on the odd-numbered items. This is your task score. Second, sum the responses on the even-numbered items. This is your relationship score.

TOTAL SCORES: Task ____ Relationship ____

## Scoring Interpretation

45-50   Very high range

40-44   High range

35-39   Moderately high range

30-34   Moderately low range

25-29   Low range

20-24   Very low range

## "Everyday Optimum Leadership: Putting Yourself in the Picture"

One of the principles of exploring leadership is personal, intentional, consistent participation in the whole development process. Explore what you already know and experience about leadership. That is what is meant by "putting yourself in the picture." Walk around "Everyday Optimum Leadership," looking at it from different sides and angles, inside and out, as you would if examining any structure. The more carefully you observe the structure, the more clearly you see what it actually is as a whole. Or, when you return from a journey, you may spend some time looking at pictures of scenes and events that made up the happening, recalling the experienced reality.

So as you move through this "Everyday Optimum Leadership gallery" step over into the picture of your life and specific service or leadership situations. Such an exercise draws conceptual input and calls for reflections on your part. Here's how it works. You will be shown a graphic requesting you to recall what element of your leadership it brings to mind. How could you serve? How do you lead? Before you are finished, you may have affirmed several strengths about yourself as well as discover new possibilities for effectiveness and satisfaction.

### Do you have a "heart for leadership"?

The word "heart" has several meanings, including the innermost center of a person, the feeling, willing, deciding capacity of being. "A Heart for leadership" could be reflected in several ways. Your leadership reflection:

- An inner sense of wholeness?
- An intentional choice to lead?
- An enduring passion for service?
- A "heart-felt" love for people?
- The capacity for hard work?
- Other_____?

## How is leadership like a lighthouse?

Most often on coastal shores, the lighthouse sends its beam of light across waters to warn of danger and to mark a safe-water entrance into the harbor. Your leadership reflection:

- Warns of danger, a cause of shipwreck?
- Persistent help in difficult times?
- Serves by its light, if it is seen and heeded?
- Other_____?

## How is leadership like a bridge?

A bridge spans some chasm of water or terrain, making it possible to cross from one side to the other. Your leadership reflection:

- Every part of the structure is essential?
- The components of the bridge are interdependent?
- Must have strength and be flexible?
- Joins the two shores, completes the journey?
- Bears traffic and payload in both directions?
- Other_____?

## As a leader, do you serve as a compass?

An instrument for showing the North so that you can steer your course in any chosen direction, or find your way from an uncertain place. Your leadership reflection:

- Helpful in new territory?
- Reliable tool, like vision?
- Sets out many choices?
- Indicates a clear direction?
- Other_____?

## When is leadership like a roadmap?

Based on surveys and measurements, a map presents routes, direction, and distance, within and between established locations. Your leadership reflection:

- Relies on the mapmaker, on previous knowledge?
- Learns from others if you pay attention?
- Establishes the whole and its related parts?
- Other_____?

## How does leadership fit into "group life"?

A group functions based on the relationship and participation of individual members, often moving toward common objectives. Your leadership reflection:

- Relationships and interdependence?
- Changing roles, with or without position?
- Multiple gifts and experience strengthen the whole?
- Other_____?

## Just, how strong is your leadership chain?

It has long been said: "A chain is only as strong as its weakest link." Is that true of you and your leadership team? Who else in your circle of influence? Your leadership reflection:

- A chain is crafted, link by link?
- Interdependency in a prominent lesson?
- Accountability, one to another?
- Weight-bearing, usually has a specific purpose?
- Other_____?

## How is leadership like team-rowing a boat?

Although we may not have personally experienced team-rowing, we have seen the images of others doing so, each person performing as part of the whole. Your leadership reflection:

- Each one has a task?
- Each task is important?
- Needs to work together, even the coxswain who does not row at all?
- Other:_____?

## Is leadership ever like white-water rafting?

A friend and I went white-water rafting, hopefully my only time ever to do so. We were told to follow five simple instructions: "Row!" "Row right!" "Row left!" "Row like crazy!"

and "Rest!" We did that, with all sorts of heroic and pitiful outcomes. Is leadership ever, or even regularly like that? Your leadership reflections:

- Importance of team effort?
- Timing is everything to success?
- Leadership has risk?
- Surprises and challenges?
- Rigorous effort is required?
- Other_____?

## Other leadership pictures/symbols?

Of course there are many other images that could be used to portray leadership. You have your own, don't you? A completely different way to portray leadership styles has been to select animals with diverse characteristics—but that's another area of study. For now, what helps you most to understand just what leadership is?

Your picture/s?_____

## Reflections:

When I think about my experiences of leadership, I see myself in different pictures given, changing leadership situations. All of the images of leadership seem to be valid. But perhaps the "bridge concept" is how I picture myself most often and comfortably. You may want to add other pictures that are most meaningful to you. After you have given thought to the visual concepts of leadership, you may see that it has opened new insights into your own behavior and experience.

—Reflect on each graphic so that you visualize elements of leadership.

—How will this add to your understanding of changing situations and leadership needs?

—What types of leaders do you work with? Are they flexible and effective?

—Are your co-workers aware of the styles and skills available to them?

## PEOPLE SKILLS
## CONNECTING WITH PEOPLE

### 1. Don't Take People For Granted.

Anytime you devalue people, you question God's creation for them.

You can never tell people <u>too often</u>, <u>too loudly</u>, or <u>too publicly</u> how much you <u>love</u> them.

### 2. Have a MAKE-A-DIFFERENCE Mindset

Anytime you don't believe you can make a difference, you won't.

    a.  Believe you can make a difference.
    b.  Believe what you share can make a difference.
    c.  Believe the person you share with can make a difference.
    d.  Believe that together you can make a difference.

### 3. Initiate Movement Toward Them

Tom Peters states, "The number one managerial productivity problem in America is quite simply, managers who are out of touch with their people and out of touch with their customers."

### 4. Look for Common Ground

All things being equal, people will do business with people they like. All things not being equal, they still will.

To relate, remember the feel, felt, found method.

    •  Respect differences in personality.

## 5.  Find the Key to Others' Lives

Emerson, "Every man is entitled to be valued by his best moments."

## 6.  Communicate from the Heart

Lincoln, "If you would win a man to your cause, first convince him that you are his friend."

- Share common experiences.

## PEOPLE SKILLS INSTRUMENTS

Rank yourself #1 hardly ever #10 most of the time

### SIX WAYS TO MAKE PEOPLE LIKE YOU

1. I become genuinely interested in other people.

    1    2    3    4    5    6    7    8    9    10

2. I smile.

    1    2    3    4    5    6    7    8    9    10

3. I remember how important a person's name is to him/her.

    1    2    3    4    5    6    7    8    9    10

4. I am a good listener. I encourage others to talk about themselves.

    1    2    3    4    5    6    7    8    9    10

5. I talk in terms of the other person's interests.

    1    2    3    4    5    6    7    8    9    10

6. I make the other person feel important and do it sincerely.

    1    2    3    4    5    6    7    8    9    10

**Add up your total is your total high, medium, or low?**

## BE AN EVERYDAY OPTIMUM LEADER

A leader's job often includes changing your people's attitudes and behavior. Some suggestions to accomplish this:

**Check out your totals . . . high, medium, low?**

1.  I begin with praise and honest appreciation.

---

    1    2    3    4    5    6    7    8    9    10

2.  I call attention to people's mistakes indirectly.

---

    1    2    3    4    5    6    7    8    9    10

3.  I talk about my mistakes before criticizing the other person.

---

    1    2    3    4    5    6    7    8    9    10

4.  I ask questions instead of giving direct orders.

---

    1    2    3    4    5    6    7    8    9    10

5.  I let the other person save face.

---

    1    2    3    4    5    6    7    8    9    10

6.  I praise the slightest improvement and praise every improvement. I'm "hearty in my approbation and lavish in my praise."

| 1 | 2 | 3 | 4 | 5 | 6 | 7 | 8 | 9 | 10 |
|---|---|---|---|---|---|---|---|---|----|

7.  I give the other person a fine reputation to live up to.

| 1 | 2 | 3 | 4 | 5 | 6 | 7 | 8 | 9 | 10 |
|---|---|---|---|---|---|---|---|---|----|

8.  I use encouragement. I make the fault seem easy to correct.

| 1 | 2 | 3 | 4 | 5 | 6 | 7 | 8 | 9 | 10 |
|---|---|---|---|---|---|---|---|---|----|

## COPING STYLE QUESTIONNAR

                A     B

1. Do you usually prefer to
   (a) take time to list the things to be done, or
   (b) just plunge in?

2. Do you usually
   (a) find waiting to the last minute nerve racking, or
   (b) prefer to do things at the last minute?

3. The word that appeals to you the most is
   (a) orderly, or
   (b) easygoing?

4. Are you bothered more by
   (a) constant change, or
   (b) routine?

5. Are you more comfortable when
   (a) dates, parties, events are planned far ahead, or
   (b) when you are free to do whatever comes up?

6. If you have to follow a schedule, does it
   (a) appeal to you, or
   (b) cramp your style?

7. Are you challenged more by
   (a) facing something unexpected and
       quickly seeing what must be done, or
   (b) following a careful plan to its conclusion?

8. Are you generally more
   (a) systematic, or
   (b) casual?

9. Are you more
   (a) punctual, or
   (b) leisurely?

Total answers for **A** and **B**

Count the number of answers you have marked **A** and enter that number in the box below the A's. Then count the number of answers you have marked **B** and enter that number in the box under the B's.

To help you see how strong your tendency is one way or the other, place an **X** on the line below, at the point that represents your score. For example, if you had 6 answers for **A** and 3 answers for **B**, then put an X at that point on the line. See below.

| Decisive / Orderly | X | Spontaneous / Flexible |
|---|---|---|
| A= 9  8  7  6  5 | | 4  3  2  1  0 |
| B= 0  1  2  3  4 | | 5  6  7  8  9 |

If you scores were to the right of the center line, then you tend to prefer to keep your options open. You are more comfortable before a decision is made, sometimes even resisting making a decision.

If you're on the left side, you are more comfortable after a decision is made. You like things to be fixed and settled.

# CHAPTER
## VII

*Optimum Attitude, Expectation, Power*
*& Success*

# ANATOMY of an EVERYDAY OPTIMUM LEADER

There are many roads that lead to success. It may not always be easy to know which one to travel, but with the right skills, planning, ambition, and energy, you can produce a direct route to the goals of your choosing. It takes:

- a heart that enables you to recognize your own qualities
- a backbone that is strong and supportive, yet flexible
- muscles that provide energy, perseverance, and health
- hands to help others and to write out your goals
- shoulders that can carry the burden of responsibility
- a brain that possesses limitless creativity and potential
- eyes that can visualize goals and possibilities
- ears that listen to your conscience and to new ideas
- a mouth that vocalizes thoughts and gives compliments
- feet that carry you on the road to success

**Henry David Thoreau said:** "If one advances confidently in the direction of his dreams, and endeavors to live life which he has imagined, he will meet with a success unexpected in common hours."

"The greatest discovery of my generation is that human beings can alter their lives by altering their attitudes of mind."

**WILLIAM JAMES**

"The only difference between stores is the way they treat their customers."

**NORDSTROMS**

## ATTITUDE CHECK-UP

- Count your blessings daily and give thanks.
- Get proper rest and exercise and start eating healthier.

- Do not let petty politics have power over your personal or professional success. Monitor what you hear, what you read, and what you say.
- Set aside personal time with family and close friends.
- Help someone less fortunate.
- Feed your spirit daily. Read and listen to uplifting books and tapes.
- Discover the motives that motivate you, and remember motivation is not permanent.
- Reflect on your victories. Rekindle the fire that helps you turn your attitude into action.
- Don't forget, the best coach with the strongest power over your performance is the coach that lives within you.

*"The happiness of a man in this life does not consist in the absence but in the mastery of the passions."—ALFRED LORD TENNYSON*

Alvin Toffler, *"The illiterate of the future are not those who cannot read or write but those who cannot learn, unlearn and relearn."*

- You are responsible for your own attitudes.
- It's not what happens to you that determine your success or failure; it's how you respond that counts.
- Things work out best for the people who make the best of the way things work out.
- How you perceive your world is the world you will live in. You can be a victim or victor.
- Winners anticipate and respond to events effectively.
- Everybody else reacts according to his or her emotional mood at the time.
- Unless you embrace and manage change, it will enslave you.
- Your greatest limitations are those you place on yourself.
- You make your own circumstances. Circumstances don't make you.

## Why change my attitude?

*"Attitude is a little thing that makes a big difference"*—*Winston Churchill*

It's amazing how your attitude can have so much to do with how successful you are in life. Yes it will make a difference to your business and work opportunities, but I've also discovered there are other ways my life has undergone some serious improvements due to some changes in attitude. This has also affected how 'successful' I am in other areas, such as my relationships, my motivation, and my overall feelings of fulfillment or happiness.

### Why is attitude important?

There is a motivational speaker named Sam Glenn that has some great ideas on why attitude is important. He offers up the following thoughts:

- Attitude is how we treat others
- Attitude is the way we approach life
- Attitude is contagious
- Attitude is how we respond to challenges
- Attitude affects our health
- Attitude affects our relationships
- Attitude is our personal trademark
- Attitude determines if we fly or fall
- Attitude creates experiences for you and others

It's difficult to recognize the importance of attitude without seeing the evidence of it in your own life.

### How do I go about changing my attitude?

Changing my attitude was the first step in taking control of my life again, and for me it started with a conscious decision.

My conscious decision to change my attitude started with making changes to how I looked and felt, and concentrating on finding solutions to move forward. Because of this decision, over the first week I began to see changes—first small ones, then larger ones as I first went to the Lord and his word for guidance then started to move one step at a time. At this point, I began to see a snowball effect—my change in attitude filtered through my family, who also were being more positive. This helped us to not only get through some tough times, but also become closer as a family.

I highly recommend reading some of the fantastic books by Justin Harold founder of 'Attitude Gear'. After starting from scratch, today Justin's business is a multi-million dollar company, with products sold throughout the world. Justin's business line initially sprung from incorporating quotes onto clothing, such as "If you think you're beaten you are!", and "It's not whether you get knocked down it's whether you get back up." He has adopted these quotes into his own life and business practices, and offers some great ideas on how we can make changes to our attitudes and enhance all aspects of our lives:

Never underestimate the power of you attitude. How you view things will have a direct impact on how you handle the next day or the next crisis. You need to make sure you are constantly checking your attitude to ensure it is on track. Consider this, if you wait for someone else to change before you allow yourself to have a winning attitude then you're giving control over to others for how you feel. Why would you allow anyone to control you in this way?

The remarkable thing is we have a choice everyday regarding the attitude we will embrace for that day. We cannot change our past . . . we cannot change the fact that people will act in a certain way. We cannot change the inevitable.

The only thing we can do is play on the one string we have, and that is our attitude . . . It has been said that life is 10% what happens to you and 90% how you react to it. And so it is with me and you . . . we are in charge of our attitudes.

**How is your attitude?** Is it having a positive or negative influence on your life? Can you make some changes to your life by changing your attitude?

**"Ability is what you're capable of doing. Motivation determines what you do. Attitude determines how well you do it."**—Lou Holtz

**Everyday Optimum Leadership and dealing with pride**

The problem with self-pride is that it is a *distancing* attitude (e.g., elitist, superior) . . . whereas pride in others (and not in YOUR 'contribution' to their greatness . . . smile) is a *bonding* attitude.

1.  **The model of God**: <u>focus on the work</u> (Gen 1.31) instead of the *worker* . . ."and God saw that *it was good*"

*Finally, brethren, whatever is true, whatever is honorable, whatever is right, whatever is pure, whatever is lovely, whatever is of good repute, if there is any excellence and if anything **worthy of praise**, let your mind dwell on these things.* (Phil 4.8)

We ARE supposed to recognize quality, and to be honest about the excellence of craftsmanship—but these are directed at the object, not at the maker.

C.S. Lewis in the *Screwtape Letters* spoke of the architect who could build a cathedral and take abject delight in it—and have the same "pride" of the cathedral regardless of who designed it or build it . . . in other words, the pride was in the quality, excellence, and beauty of the results (not of those who built it *per se*).

2.  **Try the 'we need to postpone this pride-party' tactic**:

*"So then, men ought to regard us as servants of Christ and as those entrusted with the secret things of God. 2 Now it is required that those who have been*

*given a trust must prove faithful. 3 I care very little if I am judged by you or by any human court; indeed, I do not even judge myself. 4 My conscience is clear, but that does not make me innocent. It is the Lord who judges me. 5 Therefore judge nothing before the appointed time; wait till the Lord comes. He will bring to light what is hidden in darkness and will expose the motives of men's hearts.* **At that time** *each will receive his praise from God.* [1 Cor 4, don't let your bad-pride, self-estimates get in the way of His praise!]

When you feel a self-pride-party coming up, just tell yourself that you can celebrate later—there's just too much stuff to get done right now … the longer you postpone it, the less likely it will occur 'ahead of schedule' (smile)

3.  **The model of Christ**: focus on the interests/needs of others (higher priority than reflection on your excellence, appropriate or not):

*Each of you should look not only to your own interests, but also to the interests of others. 5 Your attitude should be the same as that of Christ Jesus: 6 Who, being in very nature God, did not consider equality with God something to be grasped, 7 but made himself nothing, taking the very nature of a servant, being made in human likeness.*

[Who has time to waste in a one-person pride-party?! There is so much goodness to be done, so much growth to be achieved, so much celebrating of grace to be done!]

4.  **Exult in the things of excellence, <u>even if</u> YOU are involved (smile):**

*If anyone thinks he is something when he is nothing, he deceives himself. 4 Each one should test his own actions.* **Then he can take pride in himself,** *without comparing himself to somebody else, 5 for each one should carry his own load.* (Gal 6.4)

"With, therefore, the third person singular future verb ("he will have") and the contrast between ("in himself") and ("in someone else"), the rationale for testing one's own actions is so that "then" such a one "will have a basis for boasting in himself, and not by comparison with someone else." The warning here is not to live as spiritual people in a state of pride or conceit, always comparing one's own attainments to those of others and so feeling superior, **but rather to test one's own actions and so to minimize the possibility of self-deception. Christian feelings of exultation and congratulation** should spring from one's own actions as seen in the light of God's approval and not derive from comparing oneself to what others are or are not doing.

This pride is in one's self, as a sober reflection of actual work accomplished . . . it is the feelings of 'I feel His good pleasure in this, and I exult' Him.

### 5. Pride the warning signal:

*Pride goes before destruction, And a haughty spirit before stumbling* (Prov 16.18)

[As soon as you feel it rising, and as soon as you know you're headed for trouble, Isolate it and bring it up to Him!!!! Express your fears about falling into it—He grants help to us, when we really seek His way.]

### 6. Pride as joy/exultation in beauty and excellence is okay:

*Whereas you*[Jerusalem] *have been forsaken and hated With no one passing through, I will make you an everlasting pride, A joy from generation to generation.* (IS 60.14)

*In that day the Branch of the Lord will be beautiful and glorious, and the fruit of the earth will be* **the pride and the adornment of the survivors of Israel**. (Is 4.2)

*But be glad and rejoice forever in what I create; For behold, I create Jerusalem for rejoicing, And her people for gladness. 19 "I will also rejoice in Jerusalem, and be glad in My people;* (Is 65.18)

7. **Pride about others is something like non-embarrassment, non-shame at association—and builds community:**

*For we write nothing else to you than what you read and understand, and I hope you will understand until the end; 14 just as you also partially did understand us,* **that we are your reason to be proud as you also are ours,** *in the day of our Lord Jesus.* (2 Cor 1.13)

*We are not again commending ourselves to you but are* **giving you an occasion to be proud of us,** *that you may have an answer for those who take pride in appearance, and not in heart.* (2 Cor 5.12)

*I have great confidence in you;* **I take great pride in you.** *I am greatly encouraged; in all our troubles my joy knows no bounds.* (2 Cor 7.4)

8. **Refuse to be dominated by it!** [Be oppositional toward sin—Paul told his followers to resist being enslaved, to be 'indignant' at such attempts to enslave us]

*The* **pride of your heart has deceived you,** *you who live in the clefts of the rocks and make your home on the heights, you who say to yourself, 'Who can bring me down to the ground?'* (Ob 3)

I don't like being tricked by anything . . . I don't like being made a fool of . . . I use this against 'my old self' when I can

9. **"Pre-pride": Don't settle for such a 'cheap reward' for good effort and craftsmanship!!!:**

*Be careful not to do your 'acts of righteousness' before men, to be seen by them. If you do, you will have no reward from your Father in heaven.*

*2 "So when you give to the needy, do not announce it with trumpets, as the hypocrites do in the synagogues and on the streets, to be honored by men.* **I tell you the truth, they have received their reward in full.** *3 But when you give to the needy, do not let your left hand know what your right hand is doing, 4* *so that your giving may be in secret. Then your Father, who sees what is done in secret, will reward you. 5 "And when you pray, do not be like the hypocrites, for they love to pray standing in the synagogues and on the street corners to be seen by men. I tell you the truth, **they have received their reward in full**. 6 But when you pray, go into your room, close the door and pray to your Father, who is unseen.*

*Then your Father, who sees what is done in secret, will reward you .... When you fast, do not look somber as the hypocrites do, for they disfigure their faces to show men they are fasting. I tell you the truth, **they have received their reward in full**. 17 But when you fast, put oil on your head and wash your face, 18 so that it will not be obvious to men that you are fasting, but only to your Father, who is unseen; and your Father, who sees what is done in secret, will reward you.*

[and don't convert good works into one of these retro-actively *"Let another praise you, and not your own mouth; someone else, and not your own lips." Prov 27.2*]

[Try to avoid the subtle 'fishing for compliments' ... ]

## 10. "Convert" praise into something useful, not destructive!

*The crucible for silver and the furnace for gold, but **man is tested by the praise he receives**. (Prov 27.21)*

["thanks for the encouragement . . . can you think of something we should add to it? Someway to make it even better?]

## 11. Realize the streams of influence into your actions!

*Now, brothers, I have applied these things to myself and Apollos for your benefit, so that you may learn from us the meaning of the saying, "Do not go beyond what is written." Then you will not take pride in one man over against another. 7 For who makes you different from anyone else? What do you have that you did not receive? And if you did receive it, why do you boast as though you did not? (1 Cor 4.6ff)*

[Things are meant to be "group products"—that's why God is supposed to be a part of all YOU produce . . . ]

[When I write something great, who all is involved? My sixth grade teacher? The authors I read? The editors I have worked with?

["If you can read this, thank a teacher"

[Think how dishonest self-glory really is . . . a form of theft . . .

**12. Point to the contribution of others:**

[Thank the Lord, for the influence of _____ fill in the blank]

**13. The 'need for pride' may indicate some deep, *pathological* 'need** for a sense of significance' and therefore indicate you are 'sick' . . . so how legitimate is your pride, then?

**14. NOTE: this is not about being dishonest** . . . just being more *complete* in our assessment . . . and do not sell 'growth' short, remember . . .

[I personally don't think focusing on our sinfulness is good approach to Christ-like humility, since it could NOT have been Jesus' approach . . .

**15. Reality Check: think how stupid and silly you look, to those who can really see and/or know** . . .

[Just remember how you felt the first time you bragged about something, in front of a real expert—and were humiliated in the process . . .

[We are watched by God, and the angels, and quite possibly, the saints who have gone before us . . .

**16. My only TWO criteria for *legitimate* arrogance/pride** . . .

1. Can you speak a universe into full existence, only by sheer strength of will?
2. Can you raise yourself from the dead?

(if you answered either of these questions 'yes', then you are entitled to be 'proud' . . . smile)

**17. Convert 'proud' into 'pleased', and 'self-boasting' into 'thanks' . . .**

Recognize quality,
Celebrate growth,
Honor effort,
Rejoice with every attempt at excellence
Encourage at every incremental improvement

But don't stay too long at enjoying the beauty of your work . . . lest it become an idol and a snare . . . give thanks, and move on to the next work-of-grace and next project of beauty . . . move forward with God's fresh work in history, don't stand still and grow stale . . .

## EXPECTATION THEORY

The Expectation Theory holds that your fundamental beliefs about yourself and your world are the principal determinants of your success in life.

Fact: It is through your beliefs that you create the world you live in.

- When you change your THINKING, you change your BELIEFS.
- When you change your BELIEFS, you change your EXPECTATIONS.
- When you change your EXPECTATIONS, you change your ATTITUDES.

- When you change your ATTITUDES, you change your BEHAVIOURS.
- When you change your BEHAVIOURS, you change your PERFORMANCE.
- When you change your PERFORMANCE, you change your LIFE!

Note: You cannot change your life by trying to change your life but you can change the picture images or internal representations you hold in your mind that represent your ingrained thinking.

Core Beliefs are basic to your very being. Go through your Core Beliefs!

Key to success lies in your particular manner of thinking.

Ralph Waldo Emerson—"So far as a man thinks, he is free."

Earl Nightingale—"You become what you think about."

The Bible—"As a man thinks in his heart, so is he."

*"The quality of a person's life is in direct proportion to their commitment to excellence, regardless of their chosen field of endeavor."—VINCE LOMBARDI*

## THE POWER OF FORGIVENESS

1. Forgiveness brings an end to self-defeating behavior.

2. Forgiveness moves us out of the past.
*"Not to forgive is to be imprisoned by the past."-Robin Casarjian*

3. Forgiveness sets us free and allows us to move on.
*"To forgive is to set a prisoner free and discover that the prisoner was you."—Lewis Smedes*

4. Forgiveness makes us a better person.
*"Keeping score of old scores and scars, getting even and one-upping, always makes you less than you are."—Malcolm Forbes*

5. Forgiveness strengthens our character.
*"Strength of character means the ability to overcome resentment against others, to hide hurt feelings, and to forgive quickly."—E.H. Chapin*

6. Forgiveness makes us more loving.
*"Forgiveness is the final form of love."—Paul Tillic*

7. Forgiveness improves our mental and physical health.
*"People who replace anger, hostility, and hatred with forgiveness will have better cardiovascular health and fewer long-term health problems."—Carl Thoresen, Phd*

8. Forgiveness gives us peace of mind.
*"Forgiving those who hurt us is the key to personal peace."—G. Weatherly*

9. Forgiveness increases our wisdom.
*"Forgiveness is an essential part of wisdom."—Erwin Hall*

10. Forgiveness honors God.

## FORGIVENESS IS NOT :

1. Forgiveness does not mean you are condoning the hurtful behavior of another person.
2. Forgiveness does not mean you have to play the part of a martyr. It doesn't mean you have to continue as a victim.
3. Forgiveness does not mean that you have to pretend that everything is fine. Pain is real and forgiveness takes time.
4. Forgiveness does not mean reconciliation
5. Forgiveness—forgiving a person who has hurt you is not "wimping out" on yourself; it's taking a step toward healing.

## FORGIVENESS *IS* :

1.  Forgiveness is an attitude. It's a mindset that determines whether the hurt will continue or healing will begin.
2.  Forgiveness is a choice.
3.  Forgiveness is a process. It takes time and hard work.
4.  Forgiveness is letting go of the past. This is the hardest but the most important part of the process. We can't enjoy the present if we're stuck in the past.
5.  Forgiveness is a form of healing. It's the only thing that allows us to move on after being hurt.
6.  Forgiveness is a sign of strength. Real forgiveness requires character and courage.

### Real Forgiveness or counterfeit

"There's no way I can forgive him for what he has done. This time he knew exactly what he was doing."

So often Christians can't or won't forgive. Often the reason is that they have accepted a counterfeit forgiveness. To grasp what true forgiveness is, we must examine these common counterfeits.

### Counterfeit 1: Excusing

A speeding car driven by a drunk careens off an icy street and kills a twelve-year-old boy. If his devout parents believe they must excuse the driver because he was drunk, they will not forgive.

Excusing says, "I see you couldn't help it or didn't mean it; you weren't really to blame." That would be a lie. Forgiveness is the opposite of excusing. It reaches beyond excusing. Forgiveness acknowledges that drunken driving is inexcusable but pardons the offender anyway.

Excusing has its place, however. Many times there are extenuating circumstances. When we discover the circumstances that motivated a person, our understanding enables us to make allowances for him. But make no mistake, excusing is not forgiveness. As C.S. Lewis notes, such excusing "is not Christian charity; it is only fair-mindedness. To be a Christian means to forgive the inexcusable, because God has forgiven the inexcusable in you."

## Counterfeit 2: Minimizing the Hurt

We often deal with petty injuries by telling ourselves it doesn't matter. A child breaks her aunt's teacup and is graciously told, "That's all right, dear, I didn't like that pattern anyway."

Maturity dictates we put our injuries into proper perspective; we must be slow to take offense. The danger comes, however, when we confuse minimizing the hurt with true forgiveness. If our primary reaction when we're harmed by another is to tell ourselves feebly, *It really didn't hurt that much,* there are times it just won't wash. Rob may be able to overlook a bully punching him at the bus stop, but what does he do when gang members scar his face for life?

Unless we see the difference between acting as if the injury is minor, and pardoning one who has hurt us deeply, we will eventually find ourselves unwilling to "forgive."

## Counterfeit 3. Blind Trust

"A parent found drugs in their daughter's room so often, They can't trust her, no matter how sincerely she assures them she will stop. Does this mean they haven't forgiven her?"

Forgiving isn't the same as trusting. Even when Jesus' countrymen believed his miracles, we are told, "Jesus, on His part, was not entrusting Himself to them, for . . . He Himself knew what was in man" (John 2:24-25). There is a vast difference between forgiveness and trust; one is given, the other is earned. To someone faced with a person who perpetually breaks his promise, C.S. Lewis prescribes forgiveness: "This doesn't mean you must necessarily believe his next promise. It does mean that you must make every effort to kill every trace of resentment in your own heart—every wish to humiliate or hurt him or to pay him out."

## Counterfeit 4: Forgive and Forget

A vague anxiety gnaws at a woman who was once assaulted. Her mind replays the crime over and over. If she cannot forget, has she forgiven?

I have wondered, *When the books are opened on the great day of judgment described in Revelation 20:12, will my sins be recorded there? Has God suffered eternal amnesia? Is it impossible for Him to remember?*

No. God *chooses* not to remember my sins. The New Testament twice cites Jeremiah 31:34 (in Hebrews 8:12 and 10:17), as if to emphasize the point: "I will forgive their iniquity, and their sin I will remember no more." "Not remembering" is by no means equal to "forgetting absolutely." It means not making an effort to recall something to mind. God has not wiped out His memory banks concerning our sins; rather, He has chosen not to call them to mind against us again. I believe my sins are recorded in God's books, but over each one is written in bold red letters "Forgiven."

This distinction between forgiveness and still having painful memories is crucial. When we've forgiven, we choose not to call a person's sins to mind against him. Yet until God's healing is fully worked in our minds, the memory of the hurt and pain may overwhelm us again and again. Each time, we must write "Forgiven" over the person who hurt us. Even though we must sometimes recall painful memories for them to be healed, we must refuse to allow the enemy the luxury of salting them with bitterness. In response to our prayerful determination, God our Father supplies the strength to resist the temptation to dwell on the person's sin.

Forgiveness doesn't require forgetting, only choosing not to call to mind repeatedly while God heals the memories.

## The Genuine Article

"To err is human, to forgive is divine," Alexander Pope reminds us. So often we take our models for forgiveness from the counterfeits in the culture around us rather than from our Heavenly Father's true example.

Genuine forgiveness—pardoning an inexcusable, devastating injury—is a miracle. If we are to understand what forgiveness is, we must see it as God sees it.

God did not excuse our sins. If it would have been enough to cite our inherent weakness or some extenuating circumstances, the Father would never have sent His Son to suffer the torture of crucifixion. God does not pretend. Our pitiful pretense at independence from our Creator, our negligence, and our sins are inexcusable. The only rebuttal to sin is the bold, unilateral deed of the Offended One: "For Christ also died for sins once for all, the just for the unjust, that He might bring us to God" (1 Peter 3:18).

Neither did God meet our defiance by denying His hurt. The pain when we're deceived by a casual acquaintance is nothing compared with the pain of being betrayed by one we hold dear. Our Father refused to lessen His hurt by disowning His love for us. His love will not let us go. At the bedrock of our faith lies this assurance: "God demonstrates his own love for us in this: While we were still sinners, Christ died for us" (Romans 5:8, NIV). Forgiveness is the outworking of God's love. A trivial injury or one that's excusable needs no forgiveness. Forgiveness is pardoning one who has truly wronged us, "Just as God in Christ also has forgiven you" (Ephesians 4:32, NASB).

We can't divorce God's forgiveness of us from our willingness to forgive those who have injured us. We pray, "Forgive us our debts, as we forgive our debtors" (Matthew 6:12, KJV).

## A Decision by Faith

What is forgiveness, then? A choice—a faith decision—not to hold a sin against a person any longer. It is not based on merit, but on grace. Its prototype is the cross. We dare not confuse it with emotion.

Although feeling will eventually follow if we maintain faith's resolve despite temptations to bitterness, the feeling is not the forgiveness. It may be agony even to think about forgiving a past injury, but God will gradually enable us if we let Him. And the very decision to forgive releases God's power to restore our damaged emotions. True reconciliation is impossible without genuine repentance. Unless we acknowledge our sins, we cannot enjoy our Father's fellowship.

Then what can we do about the millions who never turn from their sins and never experience His forgiveness? If God doesn't forgive them, why must we? God's love and His desire to show mercy are constant toward the unrepentant. It's His very commitment to show mercy that allows us and draws us to come to Him. Jesus leaves no room for an unforgiving spirit, even if the offender never repents. He directs His disciples: "Love your enemies, and pray for those who persecute you in order that you may be sons of your Father who is in heaven; for He causes His sun to rise on the evil and the good, and sends rain on the righteous and the unrighteous" (Matthew 5:44-45, NASB).

The apostle Paul makes it clear that so long as we retain the right to vengeance, we can't really love our enemies (Romans 12:9). We must let go of the offense and let it be washed into the river of God's justice, that it may not pollute our springs. Paul concludes, "Do not be overcome by evil, but overcome evil with good" (vs. 21).

Christians must forgive. Jesus told the parable of a governor who owed millions to his king. But he forfeited the king's offer to forgive the debt by his own refusal to cancel a twenty dollar debt. As a result, he was imprisoned and tortured until he should pay the last penny. Jesus' application to his disciples is unmistakable: "So shall my heavenly Father also do to you, if each of you does not forgive his brother from your heart" (Matthew 18:35).

Centuries ago, George Herbert distilled the issue:"He that cannot forgive others breaks the bridge over which he himself must pass if he would ever reach heaven; for everyone has need to be forgiven."

No one said forgiving is easy. But we cannot be satisfied with quick counterfeits. Like our Father, we must face sins squarely and pardon them boldly, enabled by His grace.

## <u>SUCCESS</u>

- Success is an attitude.

- Success is a habit.

- Success is available to all who want it, believe they can have it, put their desires into action.

- Success has no secrets. The main theme is: THEY LOVE THEIR WORK.

- Wealth is a by-product of following one's passions.

- Important aspect of successful people is that they all had failures, sometimes many failures.

- Everything in life is a matter of CHOICE.

- You have to believe you can be successful before you will ever succeed.

- Your beliefs create your life experience.

- Every successful person at some point came to believe that one day they would be successful.

- What are your beliefs about success?

- For most people, failure has become a way of life. Failure is a hard habit to break.

- Success is basically no more difficult than failure. It's simply a different kind of mental programming.

## SUCCESS CONTINUED

- We're born with two fears: falling and loud noises. All other fears are acquired.

- Ask yourself why you've condemned yourself to mediocrity.

- Success is the outward manifestation of an inner focus.

- The mind is capable of anything.

- We are the creators of our own happiness or misery.

- The common theme through all success stories is a positive inner attitude.

- Subconscious mind is best represented by the image of the iceberg.

- Words are powerful agents.

- Words don't even have to be true for the mind to accept them.

- Our inner monologues program us constantly.

- The cumulative result of all our inner programming is our self-image.

- People are what they believe themselves to be.

- Picture your success. Imagine it clearly.

- What do you want? What does your version of success look like?

- What is your goal?

We always establish our goals according to our self-image. It is therefore just as hard for us to fail as to succeed. And it's just as easy for us to succeed, as it is to fail. A new self-image produces a new goal, and a new goal results in a new life. Life answered their dreams in accordance with their self-image and the faith they had in their success. You can change your self-image at any time, according to your aspirations.

Self-suggestions or affirmations should be:

1. Brief
2. Positive
3. Present tense

Mental blocks are unconscious beliefs that have been reinforced by experiences in our lives.

Both poverty and riches are the offspring of thought.

There are no limitations to the mind except those we accept.

Everyday make sure that you devote some time to reprogramming yourself, to creative visualization. Clearly imagine that you already have what you hope for, that you have reached your goals. What does your life look like? Wherever you focus your attention, wherever your energy, that is where you will grow. Most people have more imagination for conjuring up problems that prevent them from realizing their dreams than for recognizing their opportunities for success.

Change—real change—comes from the inside out. What happens in many cases is despite 10 favorable reasons, one negative reason discourages most people from trying at all. Focusing on the negative can distort our judgment and paralyze our actions.

Most people fail because they give up much too quickly. Pride or a lack of self-confidence makes people give-up too quickly. Life seems to have been designed as some sort of test. When people show they can overcome obstacles and failures with unswerving persistence and faith, life seems to lay down its weapons of opposition, and fame and fortune appear, as if charmed by their vision and strength. People are what they believe themselves to be, no more, no less. Boredom occurs when the learning curve flattens out. Successful people are ruled by passion and their hearts. They are romantics spared into action by their love of their work, their desire to do new things, to take-up new challenges and to face new risks.

## WHAT DOES *SUCCESS* MEAN TO YOU?

(Answer these questions . . . from your heart . . . not your intellect)

1. What is your personal definition of SUCCESS?

2. How will you know when you're successful?

3. How will it look and feel?

4. How close are you now?

5. What three actions can you take starting today to move closer to being successful?

# TIMELINE FOR SUCCESS

## HANDS ON

### The note:

Write a note to yourself that includes a timeline (chosen dates) when you expect to achieve a benchmark of success. Describe each of these benchmarks by defining what success will look like.

### The reminder:

Enter a reminder in a date book or calendar to review your note. Choose one of the following and answer the question(s):

1. **You succeeded as predicted.**

   a) What would you have done even better?

   b) How will you celebrate your success?

2. **Success looks different than you predicted.**

   a) What factor did you not consider when describing your benchmark of success or your timeline?

3. *You did not succeed at all.*

   a) Was the road block to success external and truly insurmountable or a shortcoming of yours?

   b) What will you do differently in the future?

## DISCOVER THE SUCCESS IN YOU HANDS ON

As an Optimum Leader presenting before a large group . . .

1.  Involve your audience in your presentation as quickly as possible.

Ask the crowd, "If you're happy to be here, say "Aye!" and immediately a chorus of "Ayes!" comes right back at you. Excellent. Now I want you to introduce yourself to four or five people sitting next to you. Go!

This opening gets the audience participating in the seminar right from the start. This puts them in an upbeat state.

2.  Commit to giving your audience more than they have any right to expect.

3.  Constantly upgrade your material to be sure that you are providing your audience with the very best of information available on your topic.

The audience doesn't just hear you but feels you.

4.  Don't memorize your speech—become it!

Speaking is a skill. Communication is power.

Speakers are a dime a dozen but communicators are rare and unforgettable.

I believe people would rather be entertained than educated. When you entertain and educate simultaneously, then you have a chance to impact mass numbers of people.

Don't just use words to speak (auditory), use the tone of your voice (emotionally), the way you move [visually), the music that plays (emotionally and auditory), have people touch each other (kinesthetically) and tell stories (laughing feels good both physically and mentally).

5.  Remember that what you're really selling are not words but feelings and emotions.

If you can incorporate music into your presentation, then do it. Anything you can use to break up your material, whether it be humor, stories, anecdotes, quotes, or audience participation, will only make your presentation that much more interesting.

6.  If you want to speak with passion, then you have to be passionate about your topic!

How do you deliver your material with passion?

By being enthusiastic about your message and then transferring that feeling of enthusiasm to your audience.

## "How does the Bible define success?"

**Answer:** When King David was about to die, he gave his son, Solomon, the following advice: "Do what the LORD your God commands and follow his teachings. Obey everything written in the Law of Moses. Then you will be a success, no matter what you do or where you go" (1 Kings 2:3). Notice that David didn't tell his son to build up his kingdom with great armies, or to gather wealth from other lands, or to defeat his enemies in battle. Instead, his formula for success was to follow God and obey Him. When Solomon became king, he didn't ask the Lord for wealth and power, but for wisdom and discernment in order to lead God's people.

God was pleased by this request and granted it, giving Solomon a wise and understanding heart, more than any man had ever had before. He also gave Solomon the things he didn't ask for—riches and honor among men (1 Kings 3:1-14). Solomon took his father's advice to heart, at least for most of his reign, and reflected on it in his writing in Proverbs: "My son, do not forget my teaching, but let your heart keep my commandments, for length of days and years of life and peace they will add to you. Let not steadfast love and faithfulness forsake you; bind them around your neck;

write them on the tablet of your heart. So you will find favor and good success in the sight of God and man" (Proverbs 3:1-4).

Jesus reiterated this teaching in the New Testament when He declared which is the greatest commandment: "Love the Lord your God with all your heart and with all your soul and with all your mind and with all your strength. The second is this: 'Love your neighbor as yourself.' There is no commandment greater than these" (Mark 12:30-31). Loving God means obeying Him and keeping His commandments (John 14:15, 23-24). The first step in this process is accepting the free gift of eternal life offered by Jesus Christ (John 3:16).

This is the beginning of true biblical success. When the gift is received, transformation begins. The process is accomplished, not by human will, but by God's Holy Spirit (John 1:12-13). How does this happen and what is the result? It happens first through trusting the Lord and obeying Him. As we obey Him, He transforms us, giving us a completely new nature (1 Corinthians 5:17). As we go through trouble and hard times, which the Bible calls "trials," we are able to endure with great peace and direction, and we begin to understand that God uses those very trials to strengthen our inner person (John 16:33; James 1:2).

In other words, trouble in life does not cause us to fail, but to walk through trouble with God's grace and wisdom. By obeying God, we gain freedom from the curses of this world—hate, jealousy, addictions, confusion, inferiority complexes, sadness without reason, anger, bitterness, unforgiveness, selfishness and more. In addition, followers of Christ (Christians) possess and display the fruit of the Spirit of God who resides in their hearts—love, joy, peace, patience, goodness, kindness, gentleness, faithfulness, and self-control (Galatians 5:22-23). We have at our disposal knowledge to know what to do and where to turn (Proverbs 3:5-6), unhindered amounts of wisdom (James 1:5), and the peace that passes understanding (Philippians 4:7).

As we grow and mature in Christ, we begin to think not only of ourselves but of others. Our greatest joy becomes what we can do for others and give to others, and how we can help them grow and prosper spiritually. Those who have risen to these heights of achievement understand true success, because a person can have all the power, money, popularity and prestige the world has to offer, but if his soul is empty and bitter, worldly success is really failure. "What good will it be for a man if he gains the whole world, yet forfeits his soul? Or what can a man give in exchange for his soul?" (Matthew 16:26).

While transformation of our inner lives is God's goal for us, He also abundantly provides good physical gifts to His children (food, clothing, houses, etc.), and He loves to do it (Matthew 6:25-33). Yet, most of us, at one time or another, focus on the gifts rather than on the Giver. That's when we regress in our contentment and joy and we quench the Spirit's transforming work within us, because we are focusing on the wrong things. That may be why the Lord sometimes limits His gift-giving to us—so we do not stumble over the gifts and fall away from Him.

Picture two hands. In the right hand there are the offer of true contentment, the ability to handle life's problems without being overcome by them, amazing peace that sees us through all circumstances, wisdom to know what to do, knowledge and constant direction for life, love for others, acceptance of ourselves, joy no matter what, and at the end of life, an eternity with the God who freely gives all these gifts. The other hand holds all the money and power and success the world has to offer, without any of what the right hand holds. Which would you choose? The Bible says, "Where your treasure is, there also is your heart" (Matthew 6:21). That which is in the right hand is the biblical definition of success.

## God's Success for YOU

One last word about success and that is most people continue to define success in terms of achieving goals, acquiring wealth, and having prestige, favor, status, and power. "Successful" people enjoy the "good life"—being financially secure, emotionally secure, being surrounded by admirers, and enjoying the fruits of their labor. Their example is emulated and their accomplishments are noticed. Most people's definitions of success only deal with the "here and now" of this life. Even in many churches today the definition of success is in terms of numbers, size, dollars and prestige.

But success is measured and defined differently by God. Again God's measure of success involves our **obedience** and **faithfulness** to Him, regardless of opposition and personal cost. His measure of success is whether or not we are being loyal to Him in our personal relationship with Him and in our life, and whether we are accomplishing **His** goals & purposes for our life. Some examples in the Bible:

Jeremiah was an absolute failure when judged by people's definition of success. For 40 years he served as God's spokesman, but when he spoke no one listened and responded. He was rejected by his neighbors, his family, the priests and prophets, friends, his audiences, and the kings. He was poor and underwent severe deprivation to deliver God's messages. He was thrown into prison and into a cistern. But in God's eyes he was a success. He faithfully and courageously proclaimed God's word and His messages, and he was obedient to his calling.

Jesus was also a failure, if you measure his life here on earth by people's measure of success. He had little in material possessions, and did not even own a home. He was rejected by most people, and was even hated by some. The religious leaders of the time despised him. Even his friends and those closest to him deserted him. He was accused and found guilty of things he did not do. He was beaten, spit on, cursed, mocked, and he suffered terribly and died the most horrible kind of death known to man at that time, death on the cross.

Measure him by the way most of us measure success, and he was a failure. But in God's eyes, the redemption and salvation of all of mankind was accomplished through His son Jesus. By God's grace and great love for you and I, He sent Jesus to pay for our sins, and now the **gift** of a restored personal relationship with God and eternal life can be ours—all because of Jesus Christ.

**"God's call is for you to be His loyal friend, to accomplish His purposes and goals for your life."—Oswald Chambers**

# CHAPTER
## VIII

*Optimum Leadership*

*Keys to:*

*Making Change*
*Setting Goals*
*Communication*
*Dealing with Stress*

# CHANGE

*"The key to change . . . is to let go of fear."*

*"I can't change the direction of the wind, but I can adjust my sails to always reach my destination."*

*"Change the changeable, accept the unchangeable, and remove yourself from the unacceptable."*

Growth from Change in 3 steps

1.  Dissatisfaction

Because of outer events or inner feelings, you decide your current situation no longer works for you.

2.  Confusion

Normally a period of confusion follows in which you challenge your old beliefs. You begin to fantasize how things could be different.

3.  Action

Someone helps you to make a decision, or an opportunity presents itself, or you manage to attain clarity. Once this happens, you take action and ideally manifest a more satisfying life.

Oh but how we resist change. Out of fear, we cling to what is and do everything within our power to keep people and things in the familiar static position. Life is change. Change is what is. If not today, then tomorrow, or next month, or next year. Everything in your life will eventually change.

Trouble starts with our desire for permanency. If you don't get what you desire, you become frustrated. If you do get what you desire, you'll still be frustrated. If your life has become lifeless, what can you fear from change? Explore your dissatisfaction, allow time for confusion and then make up your mind and with God's guidance act and create the life you have dreamed of.

## Universal principles

The broad principles of how you approach any business initiative or any activity that may require or instigate change are universal:

**Clarity in all areas**—especially of the business need for the change, of the specifics of the change, the benefits of the change, and <u>most importantly</u> the impacts of the change.

**Communication**—constant communication—two-way communication—communication that explains clearly what is change management and what is happening or not happening and why.

**Consistency**—in all aspects of the way in which you lead the change—manage the delivery—handle the communication—and ensure the realization of the benefits.

**Capability**—constant attention to the management of the tasks, activities, projects and initiatives that are delivering the capabilities into your organization that will deliver the benefits that you are seeking.

## Change and balance

## <u>DEVELOPING BALANCED CHRISTIAN LEADERS</u>

Christian organizations differ in many ways. Their size, structures, and services are shaped by internal and external forces—finances, location, personalities. But all effective Christian organizations share at least one thing in common—effectively balanced leadership. How can balanced Christian leadership be characterized? Defining leadership, much less Christian leadership is an elusive task.

Consider scriptural descriptions of Christ as leader. He is portrayed as lion and eagle but also as lamb and dove—vivid contrasts to be sure. An examination of Christ's perfect leadership qualities reveals a well-defined pattern of contrasting or balancing character traits: divine/human; compassionate/stern; traditional/revolutionary' assertive/docile. Because He was truly all things to all people, Jesus was a perfectly balanced leader.

## THE OVERLOOKED LEADERSHIP INGREDIENT

Balance is an essential, though commonly overlooked, ingredient of Christian leadership. Without complementary character and behavioral traits, how else could today's pastoral or lay leader simultaneously fulfill administrative and spiritual opportunities; be meek, yet assertive; minister to individuals via a corporate body? The effective Christian leader integrates contrasting traits and skills into a spiritual whole. To fulfill their God-given responsibilities, Christian leaders must be both active and passive. Leadership involves giving as well as taking, serving as well as directing, waiting as well as taking, serving as well as directing, waiting as well as acting. Passive and active traits must be blended to forge a servant/king leader. The true Christian leader thus reflects Jesus Christ Himself.

## ACTIVE AND PASSIVE LEADERSHIP TRAITS

Christian leadership can be meaningfully portrayed on a continuum
of character and behavioral traits ranging from active to passive:

### The Active Leader

Makes things happen

Performs tasks personally

Makes decisions unilaterally and individually

Ministers through formal programs

Talks

Orchestrates change

Teaches

Ministers through words and actions

Preaches via oratory

The Passive Leader

Delegates tasks to others

Engages in participative, shared decision making

Ministers through informal interaction

Listens

Allows change to happen naturally

Learns

Ministers through personal presence and empathy

Preaches via the Holy Spirit

Serves

In reality there is no totally active or totally passive leader, only varying blends of both traits. Leadership effectiveness is enhanced by the interplay of active and passive traits—the leader who can be many things to many people. A leader in the church or in the marketplace must certainly be capable of "makings things happen" through planning, budgeting, and program implementation. He must also possess the patience to wait for things to happen as the result of prayer or congregational mood.

Likewise, the effective leader balances individual decision making with group deliberation, personal tasks performance with delegation, and formality with informality. The well-balanced Christian leader listens as well as talks, learns as well as teaches, and emotes as well as thinks. Balance and wholeness are the keys.

## THE PROBLEMS OF UNBALANCED LEADERSHIP

Problems inevitably erupt when a leader becomes too active or too passive. Lack of balance leads to lack of effectiveness. It is unavoidable.

Overly active leaders (and their churches) are likely to experience the following interpersonal and organizational problems:

1. Premature decision making and action
2. Overwork and over-commitment
3. Precipitation of confrontations and conflicts
4. Poor interpersonal communication and congregational feedback
5. Lack of rapport building with individual church members
6. Difficulty in getting Church workers to implement decisions and programs
7. Resistance to change

The overly passive leader, on the other hand, is prone to a different set of problems:

1. Indecisive, inconsistent decision making
2. Ineffectiveness in inspiring and motivating church leaders

3   Wasting time in frequent committee meetings and informal group deliberations

4   Sloppy coordination and integration of church activities and programs

5   Congregational stagnation and preoccupation with the status quo

6   Heavy dependence on lay workers for work progress

7   Tendency for congregational problems to escalate out of control

## BALANCED LEADERSHIP—BEYOND THE INDIVIDUAL

A careful examination of the demands of balanced Christian leadership can prove frustrating. While agreeing on the need for such leadership, it is easy for one individual to feel overwhelmed at the prospect of being all things to all people. Indeed, the Christian leader who tries to be all things in all situations will probably achieve little. The answer to leadership effectiveness in a Christian organization is to expand the leadership base beyond one person. The search for balanced leadership really involves creating a leadership team or body within which active and passive orientations complement each other.

Such an interaction among a group of people who lead an organization was what Paul had in mind as he spoke of the church body: "So we, who are many, are one body in Christ, and individually members one of another" (Rom. 12:5, NASB) and "For the body is not one member, but many" (1 Cor. 12:14, NASB). Perhaps the most important, but least recognized, responsibility of an effective leader is that of developing the leadership potential of many church members or associates in the marketplace. By recognizing his own areas or strengths and weakness, the leader seeks to broaden and deepen the leadership base of his organization by gathering around him people with contrasting and complementary traits. Such differing traits provide a check-and-balance for meeting the complex demands of today's Christian organizations.

## HOW TO SET AND ACHIEVE GOALS

*It's not just setting the goals; it's being able to achieve them.*

**Four Major Obstacles:**

1. People don't realize the importance of goals.
2. People don't know how to set and achieve goals.
3. Fear of Rejection.
4. Fear of Failure.

## PROCESS TO ACHIEVE YOUR GOALS

*(You must have all 12 of these points. If one is missing, it won't work.)*

1. Desire
2. Belief
3. Write it down.
4. What are all the reasons why you want the goal?
5. Analyze your starting position.
6. Set a deadline.
7. Identify the obstacles you have to overcome.
8. Identify the additional knowledge and skills you will need to achieve your goals.
9. Identify the people whose help you will need.
10. Make a plan.
11. Visualize your goal as a reality everyday.
12. Persist.

### Going deep regarding your Goals in life

Have you set goals for where will you be in 5 years? What will you be doing? Why? Do you have a plan for your life? What are your options? What do you need to prepare? If you don't know where you are going, how will you know when you get there? How will you know what you need and how to prepare for the trip?

Christ knew the plan for His life and so knew He had to keep His life very simple. Do you have an idea of the plan God has for your life? You may have to stop and figure out how He has wired you, how you are gifted, what you are passionate about and then put this together to determine a path to follow. Once you have direction you set specific steps for the journey. With these steps in place you will be able to see exactly what you need and what will slow you down.

## Setting Specific Goals

*"I always wanted to be somebody . . . I should have been more specific."*

I read this quote by Lilly Tomlin a long time ago but it stuck with me. It made me realize that unless we are very specific about our lives and set specific goals for them, then we will look back and realize that we have not become who we could have been if we'd only planned it out. This section will be about *getting specific about your life* and who you are and setting goals to get there. We will examine your dreams, calling; passions and how to take steps to fully live them out.

## Dreams and passion

**Somewhere in you is a dream of who you could be.** It is based upon a calling that God has given you and the uniquely designed skills He has provided for you.

**Somewhere in you there is passion.** This passion is also a gift of God that, when joined with your calling and skills, enables you to make the dream a reality.

If you look back through your life you will get an inkling of **what has made you feel alive.** There are those times that you felt that this is what you were made for. They maybe went almost unnoticed because what it was you were doing felt effortless. You were just being who you are. Maybe it was constructing building with blocks, or assisting or leading at school. Maybe it was reading and understanding in a way that others didn't quite get. Possibly it had to do with caring for others or seeing a powerful snapshot moment that others missed.

Your passion, calling and dream are yours alone. They are what make you uniquely you and finding and living it is what you were made to do.

### Goal setting 101

*Where do you want to be in five years?* Think about every area of your life and write down what you want to be happening in that area at that time. (You can go to the balance living page to help you give a name to each area.) The more specific you "see" this picture the clearer you will be able to see the steps to get there.

*Write down your dream for each area of your life and be specific. These are your goals.*

Now, working backwards, what do you need to have in place in each area five years from now, four years from now, three years, two years, one year, six months, three months and one month from now to reach that goal? What do you need to do today? *Write out what you will do (your goals) by each of these specific dates.* Think through the obstacles to reaching your goals so you can think in detail about how to get around, through or overcome them. *Don't let obstacles stop you—think them through.*

Ask yourself what you need to gain in knowledge or skill to make your goals become a reality. Who do you need to ask for help and where can you find answers? Add this as steps to the goals you identified above. When you've finished as much as you can in detail for each goal, post in somewhere you will see it every day.

*Now, take daily action.* Do at least one thing every day and check it off your list.

### Don't stop there

As you grow you will discover dreams and possibilities emerging and you will need to set specific, measurable goals to make those dreams come true as well.

*Don't worry if your goals start to change as you mature in Christ.* What you had done so far has now made it possible to set new goals with Christ. Be excited about the journey, stay true to who God has made you and pursue the dreams He places in your heart with all the strength, skills, passion and calling He gives you.

## *If you fail to plan to have planned to fail*

*Life will take you where it will unless you put a rudder in and direct the course, and that rudder is called the word of God.* You have to have a direction and heading by which to steer, if you don't the currents will take you where they will and most likely you will not like where you end up.

Plan a life with direction, write down the steps and then do them one at a time. Plan for the next five years in five years you are going to be somewhere, make it a place of your choosing.

Pray for guidance as you work through this and know that the Lord is present with you. He has a plan for your life, a very specific one that ends in a goal of being with Him forever. Walk through your days with Him with a plan.

## Balance in your life

Because we have so many different parts to our lives—family and friends, career and finances health and fun, personal and spiritual growth to name just a few, maintaining

Balance among them can be very difficult. As one particular area of life begins to require more attention, we are able to give other areas less attention and life gets off kilter. Our lives also become unbalanced when we just have not given enough time and energy to areas that need it maybe because we just haven't given it much thought or haven't been able to get to it because of other pressing life issues.

Well, now is the time to start addressing the problem of balancing our lives in and for Christ.

## The Wheel of life

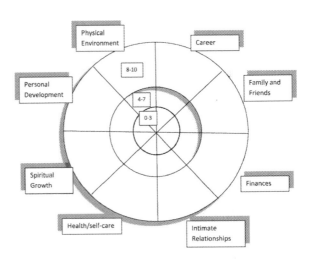

Above you will see a coaching tool called a "life wheel." We will use it to get a picture of where your life might be out of balance. If you were to rate each area listed on the wheel (and feel free to add areas or change the titles to better fit your life) on a scale from 1-10, where 1=totally unhappy and 10=great, *how would you rate your life?*

After you give each area a score, color it in up to the assigned number see whether your "wheel" is round and able to roll. Where your wheel is not round, gives you a picture of which areas of life to start to focus upon. *The goal is to bring all the areas to about the same level so it is in balance.*

A "10" in every area would be ideal, but let's shoot for an even number for now. You will find that as you start to achieve a level life wheel, even if the level is still not where you want it, your life will begin to feel more in control.

### Getting overwhelmed

As you look at your life wheel, let yourself know that Christ is right there with you. No matter what emotions arise as you look at your life, know that He is there, will bring you comfort and also knows the solutions to getting life back on track.

*You may have let your life get out of balance, but He is always able to bring your life back to center.*

And when you decide to work with Him on creating a life that glorifies Him and blesses you, He will be there with you every step of the way. In the days to come there will be more articles on bringing each area of your life with Christ back to the center. For, now, maybe it would be good to spend some time with the Lord talking over your life and what He wants it to be.

## Steps toward balance

There are a lot of items that come into play when we start to balance our lives.

—figure out **what is not working**
—determine **how it got that way**
—work on **how to fix it**

Example: *What is not working*: You've scored pretty low on health and self-care. You are finding you have less energy for daily life, you may be getting ill more often and certainly aren't looking and feeling the way you'd like.

*How it got that way*: Has not taking care of yourself been the normal way of life for you? Have circumstances changed and now you are realizing that you are no longer taking care of yourself as you used to? Or, is it that you just never gave a lot of thought to the long term ramifications of not caring for yourself and now are realizing it is time?

*How to fix it* Determine what steps you can take today, tomorrow, next week and long term to implement caring for yourself. Get a goal on paper and a date to reach it. Now, start working on it.

## What is at your core will balance your life

As you are working on re-balancing your life realize that when you know your core values and place that at the center, then you will have greater direction for your life. You will learn to balance your life wheel when your core values are at the center directing your way. Now, every area of your live will be directed by what you believe is the most important for your life. Knowing your core values makes it easy to say "no" to what doesn't fit and "yes" to what does. And that will make balancing your life so much easier.

## HOW LEADERS COMMUNICATE

Others tell. Leaders sell.
Others impress. Leaders influence.
Others try to be heard. Leaders strive to be understood.
Others explain. Leaders energize.
Others inform. Leaders inspire.
Others relay only facts. Leaders tell stories.

Great leaders are not evaluated on the length at which they speak, but on the **impact** of their message.

## PRAISE

Working with business and organizations of all kind, I hear:

- How do we increase productivity?
- How do we improve customer service?
- How do we keep people actively engaged in their work?
- How do we reduce turnover?

PRAISE matters.

A Gallup survey outlined in the book, HOW FULL IS YOU BUCKET?"
61% of American workers received no praise at work last year. The #1
reason people leave their jobs is because they feel unappreciated.

Praise matters.

When interacting with people keep these things in mind:

- Everyone needs recognition and reassurance.
- Praise gives us pride in our jobs.
- Praise generates enthusiasm and commitment.
- Praise builds loyalty.
- Praise prevents people from feeling taken for granted.
- Praise motivates us to "go the extra mile".
- Praise improves our relationships.
- Praise takes hardly any time and costs. Nothing.

## LEADERSHIP

When it comes to leadership, you can't give what you don't have.

1. Leaders determine how to get people and organizations to improve.
2. Leaders are people who, if their authority is taken away, could still achieve results.
3. Leaders continually grow through study and introspection. Learn, unlearn, and re-learn.
4. Leaders focus on how best to use their time and energy and the time and energy of others.
5. Leadership is the pursuit of more, better, faster and different.
6. Leaders

- Dare to be different
- Make sure they are asking the right questions
- Learn to act on incomplete information
- Are willing to make more mistakes

7. Leaders follow the adage, "If it isn't broken, make it better".
8. Leaders realize that performance is achieved through coaching, training and practice.
9. Leaders know that training is a necessity and that training is teaching people how to do what they are not already doing.
10. Leaders lead with enthusiasm.
11. Leaders create leaders.

## CHRISTIAN COMMUNICATION GUIDELINES

### Understanding the Concept of Guidelines

Guidelines may be considered informal "operational parameters." All types of informal parameters are used by all people on a daily basis. For example, we use such parameters to determine whether we are talking too loudly or too softly in a given social situation. No one imposes on us a precise decibel level, yet, we voluntarily adjust our speech volume so as to be most appealing, impactful, and effective in our communication to one another. This self-moderation of talking volume is a voluntary internalized guideline.

So it is intended with these Four Guidelines of Christian Communication. The precision of implementation is left up to the individual Christian. However, the intent is to follow the biblical principles (as if they were general operational parameters) from which the guidelines were derived. Each guideline is extracted from specific Bible verses, or loosely based on Scriptural injunction. God provided the biblical principles so that we might be better ambassadors of His kingdom and more loving to each other in our speech. These guidelines are meant to emphasize several specific biblical principles of speech, but not dictate the details of our discussion content.

## Principled Speech

Each "guideline" is a summary principle that ties back to a range of specific Scripture passages, though most especially Ephesians Chapter Four. The summary principles given below (One through Four) are meant to be shorthand labels encompassing a number of godly behaviors; good speech practices which edify and build up other believers and are endearing to non-Christians. Such intentional focus on the godly working of our own speech may be referred to as "principled speech." This requires the purposeful use of higher principles (biblical governance) to place parameters around what we actually utter from our lips.

## Practical Use of Principles

To make the guidelines practical in one's own life, read through the guideline labels listed below along with the Bible passages (given at the end of the article) from which they are derived. Then, go back and *memorize* the label or the name of the governing principle. Finally, share the principles with those whom are both trusted and regularly conversed with so that they may be able to help offer constructive feedback should one find himself entirely lapse on a given guideline.

Guideline Label

1.

Speak only truth

2.

Keep current

3.

Edify others

4.

Think before talking

Every time one Christian engages in conversation with another Christian, he should ask of himself, "Am I violating any of these principles?" If a guideline is being violated, or a parameter is overstepped, then one simply must change the words they use so as to conform to the guideline. It is frankly amazing what happens when one (and especially along with one's spouse) agrees to abide by each guideline, and agrees to have their words lovingly judged against these principles by the friends with which they talk. This is especially true with "speak only truth," as it requires a person to abandon using 100% words such as "you always.", or, "you never." No person is consistently "always" something, so it becomes a lie to tell someone something like, "You always exaggerate," or, "You always lie to me."

Instead, when one *speaks only the truth* they are obligated to become more precise in their speech, and therefore less unintentionally antagonistic or offensive. For example, instead of saying, "You never fill the car with gas," one may find it better to say, "Yesterday, you did not fill the car with gas; didn't we agree you would?" Consider, with regard to the accusation, "You *never* fill the car with gas," the only reply that should be expected is, "Well of course I fill up the car most of the time, you liar." However, when one becomes more specific and precise (more truthful), much of the volatile element in the situation is discharged, and an actual explanation (and probably an apology) is anticipated.

**Your Next Step**

Please contemplate taking the time to memorize each of the names of the four principles, and then attempt to apply them in your daily life. With God's grace, you may be genuinely surprised at the transformation in your speech and how people react when they converse with you.

In my own life (though I shudder to use my miserable efforts as examples), I find when I consciously apply these principles, my speech is noticeably more gracious. When I fail to think about these things before I speak, I often fail horribly. I do wonder about myself, am I more often gracious or more often failing? Adopting the regular use of the guidelines is one way by which to measure myself, to pragmatically ascertain if I see any improvement.

**The Four Guidelines of Christian Communication—*Annotated with Bible Passages***

1) Speak only truth (Ephs.4:25)

   - use no 100% words (you always . . . , you are a . . . , your style is . . . , you never . . .)no one is **always** something, making any such 100% accusatory statement into a lie
   - no name calling (name calling is the same as using 100% words—Matthew 5:22)
   - no intentional lies
   - no exaggerations (fishing stories may be exempted)

2) Keep current (Ephs.4:26,27)

   - do not let the sun set, or the church service start, before you handle a relationship problem
   - do not keep a list of offenses (1 Corinthians 13:5), handle each offense as it comes up

3) Edify the other party—do not attack them (Ephs.4:29,30)

   - the goal of instruction is love (1 Timothy 1:5)
   - the goal of discipline is to win repentance (2 Corinthians 2:6-8)
   - do not intervene in the argument between two other people (Prov. 26:17)
   - remember that we are all sinners (1 Corinthians 6:11)

4)   Think before saying anything (Proverbs 25:8)

- be slow to anger and slow to speak (James 1:19)
- hear the other person before you rebuke them (Prov. 18:13)
- be forgiving (Ephs.4:32)

## STRESS & THE OPTIMUM LEADER

Raise a glass of water and ask, "How heavy is the glass of water?"

Answer:"The weight doesn't matter. It depends on how long you try to hold it." If I hold it for a minute, that's not a problem. If I hold it for an hour, I'll have an ache in my right arm. If I hold it for a day, you'll have to call a doctor. In each case, it's the same weight but the longer I hold it, the heavier it becomes."

**That's the way it is with stress!**

If you carry your burdens all the time, sooner or later, as the burden becomes increasingly heavy, you won't be able to carry on. As with the glass of water, you have to put it down for a while and rest before holding it again. When we're refreshed, we can carry on with the burden. So before you return home tonight, put the burden of work down. Don't carry it home. You can pick it up tomorrow. Whatever burdens you're carrying now, let them down for a moment if you can.

Relax! Pick them up later after you've rested. Life is short! Enjoy it!

## STEPS TO LOWER STRESS

- Set personal goals to give yourself a sense of purpose.

- Manage time by setting priorities and eliminating unrealistic goals. Don't put things off. Delegate whenever you can.

- Make time to play, have fun and recharge. Keep time free for yourself.

- Count your blessings. Make thankfulness a habit.

- Use positive self-talk.

- Eat right.

- Get enough sleep (8 hours).

- Simplify.

- Forgive. Grudges are too heavy to carry around.

- Practice optimism and positive expectancy. Hope is a muscle—develop it.

## What does the Bible say about overcoming stress?

In today's world it is virtually impossible to avoid stress. Almost everyone is carrying some amount of it, in varying degrees. Many find it increasingly difficult to simply survive in the world we live in. In desperation, people are seeking relief for their problems through any remedy they can find. Our culture is inundated with self-help books, therapists, time-management workshops, massage parlors, and recovery programs (to name just the tip of the iceberg). Everyone talks about returning to a "simpler" way of life, but no one seems to even know exactly what that means, or how to attain it. Many of us cry out like Job, **"The churning inside me never stops; days of suffering confront me." (Job 30:27)**.

Most of us are so used to carrying the burden of stress, we can scarcely imagine our lives without it. We think it is simply an unavoidable part of living in the world. We carry it like a hiker trudging out of the Grand Canyon with a huge pack on his back. The pack seems to be a part of his own weight, and he can't even remember what it was ever like to not be carrying it. It seems that his legs have always been that heavy and his back has always ached under all that weight. Only when he stops to rest for a moment and takes off his pack does he realize just how heavy it really is, and how light and free he is without it.

Unfortunately, most of us cannot just unload stress like a backpack. It seems to be intrinsically woven into the very fabric of our lives. It lurks somewhere beneath our skin (usually in a knot between our shoulder blades). It keeps us up late into the night, just when we need sleep the most. It presses in on us from all sides. Yet, Jesus says, **"Come to me all you who are weary and burdened, and I will give you rest. Take my yoke upon you and learn from me, for I am gentle and humble in heart and you will find rest for your souls. For my yoke is easy and my burden is light." (Mt. 11:28-30)**.

Those words have touched the hearts of many, yet they are only words that merely sound comforting and are in essence, worthless, unless they are true. If they are true, how can we apply them to our lives and walk free from the burdens that weigh us down so badly? Perhaps you are responding, "I would love to do that if only I knew how!" How can we receive rest for our souls?

## COME TO ME . . .

The first thing we must do to be free from our stress and our worry is to come unto Jesus. Without Him, our life has no real purpose or depth. We simply run from one activity to another, seeking to fill our lives with purpose, peace, and happiness. **"All man's efforts are for his mouth, yet his appetite is never satisfied." (Ecc. 6:7)**. Things haven't changed much since the days of King Solomon. We work ourselves to the bone for the things we desire, only to crave more.

If we do not know our real purpose in life; our reason for existing, life is very meaningless indeed. Yet, God created each of us with a special purpose in mind. There is something that needs to be done on this earth that can only be done by you. Much of the stress that we carry springs from the fact that we don't know who we are or where we are going. Even Christians, who know that ultimately they are going to heaven when they die, are still anxious in this lifetime because they do not really know who they are in Christ and who Christ is in them. No matter who we are, we are bound to have tribulation in this life. It is unavoidable, but having trouble in this life is not the issue anyway. <u>The real issue is how we react to it.</u> That is where stress is born. The trials we face in this world will either break us or make us strong.

*"I will show you who he is like who comes to me and hears my words and puts them in to practice. He is like a man building a house who dug down deep and laid the foundation on rock. When a flood came the torrents struck that house but could not shake it because it was well built." Luke 6:48.* Jesus didn't say that once we built our house on the rock that everything would be perfect. No, He said that a flood came in torrents smashing against the house. The key is that the house was built on the rock of Jesus, and the rock of *putting His words into practice.* Is your house built on Jesus?

Did you dig your foundation deep into Him, or was the house hastily erected? Is your salvation based on a prayer you prayed once or is it growing out of a committed relationship to Him? Do you come to Him every day, every hour? Are you putting His words into practice in your life, or do they lie there like dormant seed?

*"Therefore, I urge you, brothers, in view of God's mercy, to offer your bodies as living sacrifices, holy and pleasing to God—this is your spiritual act of worship. Do not conform any longer to the pattern of this world, but be transformed by the renewing of your mind. Then you will be able to test and approve what God's will is—His good, pleasing and perfect will." Romans 12:1-2*

Until you have fully committed yourself to God, until your foundation is dug deep into Him, you will never be able to discern what His perfect will is for your life. When the storms of life come, as they are bound to do, you will only worry and fret and walk around with an ache in your back. <u>Who we are under pressure reveals who we really are.</u> The storms of life wash away the thin veneer that we present to the world and expose what lies in our heart. God, in His mercy, allows the storms to hit us so we will turn to Him and be cleansed of the sin that we were never able to perceive in times of ease. We can either turn to Him and receive a soft heart in the midst of all our trials, or we can turn away and harden our heart. The hard times in life will either make us pliable and merciful, full of faith in God, or angry and brittle, full of doubt and unbelief.

## FEAR OR FAITH?

*"If God is for us, who can be against us?" (Romans 8:31).* Ultimately, there are only two motivating factors in life: fear or faith. Until we truly *know* that God is for us, loves us, cares about us personally and hasn't forgotten us, we will base our life's decisions on fear. All fear and worry stems from a lack of faith in God. You may not think you are walking in fear, but if you aren't walking in faith, you *are*. Stress is a form of fear.

Worry is a form of fear. Worldly ambition is rooted in a fear of being overlooked—of being a failure. Many relationships are based on the fear of being alone. Vanity is based on a fear of being unattractive and unloved. Greed is based on a fear of poverty. Even anger and rage are based on the fear that there is no justice, no escape, no hope.

Fear breeds selfishness, which is the exact opposite of God's character. Selfishness breeds pride and indifference to others. All of these are sin and must be dealt with accordingly. Stress arises when we try to serve both ourselves (our fears), and God at the same time (which is impossible to do). **"Unless the Lord builds the house, its builders labor in vain . . . In vain you rise early and stay up late, toiling for food to eat." (Psalm 127:1-2).**

The Bible says that when everything else is stripped away, only three things remain: faith, hope, and love—and that love is the greatest of the three. Love is the force that drives out our fear. *"There is no fear in love but perfect love drives out fear, for fear has a torment. The one who fears is not made perfect in love." (1 John 4:18).*

The only way we can get rid of our anxieties is to look them in the eye and deal with them at the root. If we desire for God to make us perfect in love, we will have to repent of every bit of fear and worry that we have clung to instead of Him. We may not like to face some of those things that are in us, but we must if we are ever to be free from them. If we are not merciless with our sin, it will be merciless on us. It will drive us like the most wicked of slavemasters. Worst of all, it will keep us from communion with God.

Jesus said in *Matthew 13:22*, *"The one who received the seed that fell among the thorns is the man who hears the word, but the worries of this life and the deceitfulness of wealth choke it, making it unfruitful."* It is extraordinary what tremendous power there is in even the littlest things to distract us from God. We must stand our ground, and refuse to let the thorns choke out the seed of the Word.

The devil knows that if he can distract us with all the cares of this world, we will never be a threat to him or fulfill the call that is on each our lives. We will never bear any fruit for the kingdom of God. We will fall far below God's intended place for us. Yet, God wants to help us to do our best in every situation that we face. That is all He asks—that we trust in Him, put Him first, and do the best we can. After all, most other circumstances that we worry about are beyond our control anyway. What a waste of time worrying is! If we only worried about the things that we have any direct control over, we would reduce our worrying by 90%!

Paraphrasing the Lord's words in **Luke 10:41-42**, Jesus is saying to each one of us, *"You are worried and upset about many things, but only one thing is needed. Choose what is better and it will not be taken from you."* Isn't it wonderful that the only thing that cannot ever be taken from us, is the only thing we really need anyway? Choose to sit at the Lord's feet and listen to His words and learn from Him. By so doing, you are putting a deposit of true riches into your heart, *if* you guard those words and put them into practice.

If you are not daily spending time with Him and reading His Word, you are opening the door of your heart to the birds of the air who will steal the seeds of life deposited there, and leave worry in their place. As for our material needs, they will be taken care of when we seek Jesus first. **"But seek ye first the kingdom of God and his righteousness; and all these things will be added unto you. Take therefore no thought for the morrow: for the morrow will take thought for the things of itself. Sufficient unto the day is the evil thereof."** Matthew 6:33.

God has blessed us with a most powerful tool; His Living Word, the Bible. If used properly, it is a spiritual sword; separating our faith from our fear, drawing a clean line between the holy and the vile, cutting away the excess and bringing forth the repentance which leads to life. Stress merely indicates an area of our life where our flesh is still on the throne. The life that is totally submitted to God is marked by the trust born out of a thankful heart.

*Peace I leave with you, my peace I give unto you: not as the world giveth, give I unto you. Let not your heart be troubled, neither let it be afraid. John 14:27 (KJV).*

## TAKE MY YOKE UPON YOU . . .

How it must grieve God to see His children walking around in such misery! The only things we really need in this life, He already purchased for us at Calvary through a terrible, agonizing, and lonely death. He was willing to give everything for us, to make a way for our redemption. Are we as willing to do our part? Are we willing to lay our lives down at His feet, and take His yoke upon us? For if we do not walk in *His* yoke, we are bound to walk in another.

We can either serve the Lord who loves us, or the devil who is bent on destroying us. There is no middle ground, nor is there a third option. Praise God that He made a way out of the cycle of sin and death for us! When we were completely helpless against the sin that raged in us and compelled us to run from God, He had mercy on us and ran after us, though we only cursed His Name. He is so tender and patient with us, not willing for even one to perish. **A bruised reed he will not break,**

**and a smoldering wick He will not snuff out. (Matthew 12:20)**. Are you bruised and broken? Is your flame dimly flickering? Come to Jesus *now!*

*"Come all you who are thirsty, come to the waters; and you who have no money, come buy and eat! Come, buy wine and milk without money and without cost. Why spend your money on what is not bread and your labor on what does not satisfy? Listen, listen to me, and eat what is good, and your soul will delight in the richest of fare. Give ear and come to me; hear me that your soul may live!"* Isaiah 55:1-3.

## BLESS THE LORD, O MY SOUL

When all is said and done, there are still times when we all face incredibly difficult circumstances that have an awesome power to destroy us. The best way to counteract stress in those times is to begin to praise God and thank Him for His countless blessings in our lives. The old adage "count your blessings" really is true. In spite of everything, there are so many blessings woven throughout our lives that many of us do not even have the eyes to see them.

Even if your situation seems hopeless, God is still worthy of all your praise. God delights in a heart that will praise Him no matter what the bankbook says, our family says, our time schedule says, or any other circumstance that would try to exalt itself against the knowledge of God. As we praise and bless the name of the Most High, everything else in this world begins to pale and fade away against the sheer loveliness of who He is.

Think of Paul and Silas, feet bound in stocks in a dark prison with a jailer standing guard over them. **(Acts 16:22-40)**. They had just been severely flogged, ridiculed and attacked by a huge crowd of people. Instead of fearing for their lives, or becoming angry at God, they began to praise Him, singing out loud, careless of who might hear or judge them. As they began to praise Him, their hearts were soon overflowing with the joy of the Lord.

The song of those two men who loved God more than life itself began to flow through them like a river of liquid love into their cell and out into the entire prison. Soon, there was a flood of warm light bathing the whole place. Every demon there began to flee in utter terror of that praise and love to the Most High. Suddenly, an amazing thing happened. A violent earthquake shook the prison, the doors flew open, and *everybody's* chains came loose! Praise God! Praise *always* brings freedom, not only for ourselves, but for those around us who are bound up as well.

We must get our mind off of ourselves and the problems we face and onto the King of Kings and the Lord of Lords. One of the miracles of a life transformed by God is that we can be thankful always, and praise Him in all situations. This is what He <u>commands</u> us to do, for He knows better than we do that the joy of the Lord is our strength. God does not owe us anything, but He has made a way for us to receive every good thing anyway, because He loves us! Is that not a reason for celebration and thanksgiving?

*"Though the fig tree does not bud and there are no grapes on the vines, though the olive crop fails and the fields produce no food, though there are no sheep in the pen and no cattle in the stalls, yet I will rejoice in the Lord, I will be joyful in God my Savior. The Sovereign Lord is my strength; he makes my feet like the feet of a deer and enables me to go on the heights." Habakkuk 3:17-19.*

*"Bless the Lord, O my soul: and all that is within me, bless his holy name. Bless the Lord, O my soul, and forget not all his benefits: Who forgiveth all thine iniquities; who healeth all thy diseases; Who redeemeth thy life from destruction; Who crowneth thee with lovingkindness and tender mercies; Who satisfieth thy soul with good things; so that thy youth is renewed like the eagle's." Psalm 103:1-5 (KJV).*

Won't you take some time right now to re-commit your life to the Lord? If you don't know Him, ask Him into your heart. If you do know Him tell Him that you want to know Him better. Confess your sins of worry, fear and lack of faith and tell Him that you want Him to replace those things with faith, hope and love. No one serves God by his own strength—we *all* need the power and the strength of the Holy Spirit to permeate our lives and continually lead us back to the precious cross, back to the Living Word. You can make a fresh start with God, starting this very minute. He will fill your heart with a brand new song, and joy unspeakable and full of glory!

*"But unto you that fear my name shall the Sun of righteousness arise with healing in his wings; and you shall go forth, and grow up (leap) like calves released from the stall." Malachi 4:2. (KJV)*

The bottom line in all of this is the fact that you and I are on a journey, I need to trust in God, His word and the power of the Holy Spirit every hour of every day. By doing so I can live the life of an Everyday Optimum Leader with a lot less stress and be of greater use to my Lord to help build His Kingdom.

## CHAPTER
## IX

*Knowing discouragement*
*Knowing failure*
*And 11 tips to move beyond*

# WAYS TO FAIL AS A LEADER

1. Not listening . . . Impact: Creates indifference, hostility, and miscommunication.

2. Fostering confusing through lack of vision or clear purpose . . . Impact: Poor focus, little coordination, haphazard planning.

3. Not trusting or believing in the capacity of others . . . Impact Creates resentment, weakens employee's self-confidence.

4. Playing politics . . . Impact: Poor cooperation, suspicion.

5. Not creating time for dialogue, sharing information . . . Impact: Low synergy.

6. Not recognizing diversity . . . Impact: Treating everyone the same, communicating poorly with others, anger, resentment, misunderstanding.

7. Stealing credit versus giving credit to others . . . Impact: Generates anger and resentment, de-motivates, and weakens trust.

8. Fostering the impression that someone doesn't matter, Isn't valued . . . Impact: Creates apathy, low confidence, resentment, powerlessness.

9. If it isn't broke, don't fix it . . . Impact: Lack of passion, low aspirations, missed opportunity, poor quality focus.

10. Perseverance poverty . . . Impact: No stick-to-it-ive-ness," no follow through, lack of commitment, indifference, and cynicism.

## The Optimum Leader failure and Discouragement

Have you ever been discouraged? What a dumb question, if you have ever tried to accomplish anything in life and failed you have been discouraged. So now, as an Everyday Optimum Leader what do you do? How do you deal with it? Some of us use excuses such as putting blame on another person for our failure. "Because "they," did not follow up this whole thing fell apart. Or we might resign to saying, "under these conditions and circumstances it was bound to fail." Well, a key element regarding living as an Everyday Optimum Leader is to, "RISE ABOVE THE CIRCUMSTANCES." The fact of the matter is the circumstances for the most part will always be there you need to make the decision if you want to live under them or above them. And living above them is accomplished through following God's word and being lead by His Spirit.

All of us become discouraged occasionally. That is simply a part of being human. One should not feel that discouragement is intrinsically sinful for it is not. That is evidenced by the fact that even our Lord sometimes became discouraged. For example, the prophet Isaiah represents the coming Messiah as saying, "I have labored in vain, I have spent my strength for nothing and vanity; yet surely the justice due to me is with Jehovah, and my recompense with my God" (Isaiah 49:4). One cannot read Psalm 22:6-13 without detecting a note of distress in the Savior's depiction of humanity's rejection of Him. And do you not recall the apostle's comment at the conclusion of Christ's great, but difficult, discourse on the bread of life—"Upon this many of his disciples went back and walked no more with him" (John 6:66). Subsequently, the Lord longingly asked, "Would you also go away?" or as the Greek text literally suggests, "You won't leave me too, will you?" The question aches with discouragement.

The Master's men were also discouraged from time to time. Following Jesus' death, and yet before His resurrection, the disciples were distressed, for they believed the Lord's cause had been buried with His body! Their discouragement, however, was soon to be turned into elation! Even the usually vibrant Paul could have fitful moments when reflecting upon how far short he fell of the divine ideal (Romans 7:24). And so, if the Savior and His disciples were not without distress on occasion, surely we cannot expect to be. It is not the fact that one becomes discouraged that is so crucial; rather, *it is how he reacts to and handles the distress that is important.*

## Discouragement vs. Depression

Exactly what is discouragement? And how does it relate to what we call "depression"? "Discouragement" might be defined in the following way. Discouragement is a *temporary* feeling of disappointment or disheartenment, resulting from a disadvantageous turn of events—physical, material, social, emotional, or spiritual. Note the emphasis upon "temporary." If one does not address the source of his discouragement, and come to grips with it, his distress may evolve into "depression."

By way of contrast, "depression" may be defined as a *protracted period of despondency* that greatly curtails, or even destroys, one's ability to function as a healthy and happy person. If depression is not properly and urgently addressed by the Christian, with the solutions to one's problems being sought in the Word of God (whenever possible), the tragic situation can result in spiritual stagnation, overt apostasy from the faith, and sometimes, even suicide.

## Biblical Cases

The Bible contains a number of examples of people who lapsed into the state of spiritual terror that may aptly be described as "depression." Let us briefly reflect upon a few of these cases.

1. Saul, of Old Testament fame, was a man who started brilliantly as Israel's first king. He was robust and courageous and hence had the admiration of his subjects. Eventually, though, he imbibed the spirit of disobedience, and so was informed by God's prophet that the kingdom would ultimately be torn from his grasp. We are told that "the Holy Spirit departed from Saul, and an evil spirit from God troubled [terrified,] him" (1 Samuel 16:14). The latter expression simply means that God *allowed Saul to reap the mental consequences*

*of his rebellious disposition.* The king was given to fits of prolonged depression wherein he repeatedly attempted to kill David. Finally, he took his own life!

2. Judas is another example of a man so immersed in depression as a consequence of his betrayal of the Son of God that he committed suicide (Matthew 27:3-5).

More on the positive side consider these cases:

1. Job's religious motives were challenged by Satan, and the hateful Deceiver was allowed to inflict the patriarch. Job lost his children, his wealth, and his health, and still he courageously refrained his lips from sinning (Job 1:13-2:10). When, however, his three so-called friends arrived and sat down, mourning for seven days [thus treating him as one already dead!], it was more than the great patriarch could stand, and he lapsed into a state of deep depression. He wished that he had been born dead, or that he might have died at birth (Job 3). Happily, though, eventually he was able to climb out of his distress and, after repentance, was restored to the Lord's favor.

2. Similarly, the noble Jeremiah, known as the weeping prophet, because he was so ill-treated by evil Israel, gave way to the pangs of depression and cursed the very day of his birth (Jeremiah 20:14). But he too was able to overcome that depth of grief.

## Causes and Cures

In order to deal with discouragement and/or depression, one must first be able to correctly diagnose the source of his problem. Second, he must be aware of the options available for the remedial solution to his problem, or if there is no immediate solution, he must concentrate his attention upon that Source of strength that will allow him to accept the situation as it is, and even to grow thereby. As noted earlier, the causes of depression may be classified under various headings. Let us give our attention to several of these.

Our aim here is to address those categories of depression that have *spiritual* bases, and thus can be remedied with applications from the Scriptures. And these are far more numerous than many are willing to admit. Unfortunately, many people today are looking for the quick-fix, "pill" solution.

1. **Physical**—Let us suppose a man is involved in a terrible car accident and he becomes paralyzed from the neck down. How shall he handle this misfortune? First, he may need to come face-to-face with the fact that he simply cannot change the situation. Second, he could become a self-pitying, depressed recluse and finally waste away. On the other hand, he might summon the courage to be a balanced, productive person, who even by his handicap is able to marvelously glorify God! There are numerous examples in this latter category that have influenced thousands by their courage and determination.

How should one react if he discovers he has a most serious, possibly fatal, illness? He may, with firm determination, attempt to fight the illness, and perhaps he will win. If he sees that the battle is being lost, he must realistically acknowledge that death eventually claims us all. It is the price we pay for humanity's involvement in sin (Romans 5:12). But anger, frustration, and depression (though perhaps initially natural) will not remedy the situation. The believer must fortify his spirit with the fact that those who die "in the Lord" are exceedingly blessed (Revelation 14:13), and they will enter a state that is "very far better" (Philippians 1:23).

2. **Material**—How should one respond who has suffered a severe financial blow? If the treasury of his heart (Matthew 6:21) has been filled with materialism, he may not be able to handle the losses. Look at where we are today regarding the economy. When the stock market crashed in 1929, some were so crushed they committed suicide! One who trusts in God for all things might (after a brief emotional adjustment) be constrained to say with Paul, "we brought nothing into the world, for neither can we carry anything out; but having food and covering we shall therewith be content" (1 Timothy 6:7-8). Of course it would not be sinful to vigorously work for the

restoration of that which was obtained honorably; hard work is the eraser of "hard luck." Too, it is possible that one may have to face the fact that he simply will not always be able to live at the high standard to which many have become accustomed. God has never promised economic luxury to His people; only daily bread. In any case, depression has never solved a financial problem!

**Social**—Many a poor soul has descended into the depths of depression when forsaken by a dear friend. Unrequited love has been the undoing of some. How does a young bride-to-be deal with the heartache of being forsaken by her fiancée just hours before the wedding ceremony? Of course she will be deeply hurt, but she must recognize several things.

There is One who will never forsake the Christian (Psalm 118:8; 2 Timothy 4:16-17).

The providence of God may be at work; the Lord may have someone better in mind for His young saint.

In spite of this tragedy, in due time it certainly is possible that this person could live a wonderfully happy and fruitful life—even though single.

The point is this: one must never give in to depression; the human spirit must fight back.

**Emotional**—How does one cope with the tragic death of a spouse, or a child? Surely such a heart-breaking blow must be almost more than one can bear. True, but these things are a part of the world in which we live, and they *will continue to occur* whether we learn to deal with them or not! In such dark hours of adversity the child of God may reflect upon several things. First, if the loved one was in a state of innocence (e.g., a child) or was faithful to the Lord, we must not sorrow in the way those without hope do (1 Thessalonians 4:13). There is recognition and association beyond death (Genesis 25:8; 2 Samuel 12:23; Matthew 8:11; 17:3; Luke 16:9,19ff). Second, even if the deceased died outside of Christ, depression will not bring back that loved one! This is a hard fact that must be faced.

Moreover, we can be comforted by the fact that God is aware of our grief (Psalm 56:8; 103:13; 2 Kings 20:5) and He is the God of all comfort (2 Corinthians 1:3), who is able to help us bear the burden (Psalm 55:22). Finally, all of our heartaches will be removed in heaven (Revelation 21:4). We must thus take courage and bear up!

**Spiritual**—Much of our discouragement/depression is the consequence of our guilt, resulting from sinful conduct or the neglect of spiritual responsibility. This was the problem of Saul and Judas mentioned earlier. Some charge that preachers are always trying to make people feel guilty. The fact is, it is the responsibility of God's preaching servants to proclaim the truth—in a loving manner, yes; but forcefully nonetheless. If that burdens some with guilt, so be it. There is a way to take care of that— repent of sin!

The psalmist described the grief that can attend the guilty conscience. Listen to him:

"Have mercy upon me, O God; for I am withered away: O God, heal me; for my bones are troubled. My soul also is sore troubled ? I am weary with my groaning; every night I make my bed to swim with tears; I water my couch with my tears. My eyes waste away because of my grief" (Psalm 6:2-7). The weary soul who is laboring under the heavy weight of a guilty conscience has a way out. He can repent of his evil (which demands undoing that wrong, as much as humanly possible) and ask for God's forgiveness.

The person who is not a Christian may submit to the Lord's saving plan and receive remission of sins (Acts 2:38), being assured that his evil has been blotted out (Acts 3:19,) and remembered no more by the Creator (Hebrews 8:12).

The unfaithful child of God may repent and pray, and have the same assurance. It is true that the consequences of sin may extract a severe price for years to come [an adulterous relationship may have to be severed;

imprisonment may be required for a crime committed], but with God's help, such a life need not be enslaved by overwhelming depression.

## Concluding Counsel

If one is to learn how to conquer, or at least control, depression, there are certain attitudes he must learn to identify and avoid—attitudes that have a tendency to nurture the moods in which depression can flourish. Let me mention a few of these matters in brief.

1. Too many of us are, to a degree, self-centered. We are constantly wondering why someone did not speak to us, or we are aggravated because *our* needs are not being addressed by the church. The truth is, if many would get busy with the needs of others, they would not have the time for preoccupation with personal problems. <u>Remember this, even from the cross the Savior was thinking of others!</u> "Other Centered Focused."

2. What we constantly think about, we tend to become (Proverbs 23:7; Mark 7:21-23). Those who focus almost continuously upon the negative—how bad I feel, how hard I have it, woe is me!—tend to dredge themselves deeper into depression. We must learn to concentrate upon more positive things, to count our blessings. Pleasant thoughts and words are "sweet to the soul and health to the bones" (Proverbs 16:24).

3. A preoccupation with the trivial along with a corresponding lack of spiritual activity can create a void in one's life that allows depression to move in. An idle mind and life truly are the devil's workshop.

4. Sometimes those who are depressed have a tendency to seek out the companionship of others with similar problems. These persons thus feed upon one another's distresses, and actually end up destroying each other. When you are troubled, associate with those who can build you up.

5. Do not be intimidated by the opinions of your critics. You can never live up to the expectations of some people, and you will be under a constant strain if you try. <u>Simply attempt to please God and be aware of the fact He understands your frailties and He will lovingly bear with you as you grow.</u> In short this is at the core of an Everyday Optimum Leader.

6. Do not expect instant, magical solutions to your problems. God is not going to perform miracles and make your life on earth a present "heaven." By following the instructions of the Scriptures, be patient and work to solve your difficulties.

7. Finally, one must <u>leave the unsolvable to God.</u> Trust Him no matter what. Learn to be content no matter how dire your conditions are (Philippians 4:11-13). Recognize the fact that tranquility of mind does not depend upon the external, <u>but upon the internal.</u> Remember "it all starts on the inside." Live it, show it, be it.

## OPTIMUM LEADERSHIP TIPS

### Tip # 1

Henry Miller once wrote: "No man is great enough or wise enough for any of us to surrender our destiny to. The only way in which anyone can lead us is to restore to us the belief in our own guidance." For the Christian my own guidance is based on God's word in my life.

A leader motivates and directs and runs and guides and leads and restores. A leader does more than lead—they restore to people their belief in their own guidance.

How Do You Become a Leader?

1. Help people think better of themselves. Reasons why it's vital for you to help people think better of themselves:

First, what people think about themselves is the single most important factor in their success: their personalities, their actions, their feelings, how they get along with others, how they perform at work, their beliefs, their aspirations, even their talents and abilities are controlled by their self—images.

People act like the kind of persons they imagine themselves to be.

## STAYING YOUNG YOUR WHOLE LIFE

### Tip # 2

Have you ever noticed that while some people in their 80's still seem youthful, others appear old at 40?

The difference is one of ATTITUDE.

*"As a man thinks in his heart, so is he." Prov.23:7*

People don't have to get old unless they choose to do so. Instead of asking, "How old are you?" we should ask, ***"HOW MANY YEARS HAVE YOU LIVED?"***

I believe we have a responsibility to <u>be our best, do our best, and to look our best.</u>

### Some Steps We Can Take:

1.  Keep Learning.

Don't settle for what you already know. Never accept things as they are. Keep gaining knowledge. As we learn, we stop worrying and fretting. We then gain energy and a sense of anticipation.

> *"To get the body in tone, get the mind in tune."*
> *– ZACHARY T. BERCOVITZ*

Everything in our body flows differently when we have a sense of assurance, contentment, and quietness in our inner being.

Gain knowledge about valuable things. If we cease to learn, we get into "rut living" and "rat race" which leads to aging. Learning will keep your mind fertile and young.

2. Keep Loving

Love causes energy to flow in your life—people who love remain youthful in their spirit for the simple reason that they have anticipation and excitement.

If we don't love or feel loved, we will quickly start to age. Therefore, in order to stay young, fall in love everyday and learn to let somebody love you.

3. Keep Laughing

Laughter affects every cell in our bodies. When we laugh, our immune system is stimulated, as is our creativity.

Physicians tell us that "a joyful heart is a good medicine".

Let the child out that is inside of each of us. Express what you feel and enjoy life. Take yourself less seriously. Find reasons to rejoice.

4. Keep Letting Go (of emotional baggage)

Stop living in the past clinging to old hurts.

We will age quickly if we do not learn to leave behind the past will all of its regrets, disappointments and heartaches. God wants us to focus our mind on the present and the future. Give Him our past burdens. Learn to forgive others and ourselves. Be willing to stop living in the past.

5. Keep Desiring (for better things)

Don't give up your dreams or you will start aging.

I learned that I am the most motivated and content when I am working toward a goal or looking forward to enjoying a desire. Anticipation keeps us young. Never settle for goals that are too small or too safe. Make big plans and dreams—big enough that they won't come to fruition without God's help. Keep in mind that God has wonderful plans for each one of us. It will be exciting and you will discover that you have more energy, more stamina and more faith than ever before.

6. Keep Leaning (on God)

Prov. 3:5-6: "Trust in the Lord with all your heart and do not lean on your own understanding. In all your ways acknowledge Him and He will make your paths straight."

We don't have to age because of troubles, trials or heartaches.

Will your body age? YES. But that doesn't mean you have to become old in our mind, in your spirit, or in your heart.

## THE UNEXAMINED LIFE BECOMES A LIABILITY

### Tip # 3

Dreams are the power behind our motivation and God's cultivation is the tool He give us to unlock them.

Questions:

1. How much of a self-starter are you?

2. What are your passions?

3. Have you ever decided to learn a new skill and then gone out and done it on your own?

4. Did you have an idea about creating or building something from scratch and you didn't stop until it was done?

These are the kind of things entrepreneurs do. We don't even give is a second thought. Part of it is that ability to visualize the end result. Hold it in your mind and keep moving toward your goal. When set back come, you don't let them beat you down. Just pick up and start over again. Just keep going in that direction and you will reach your goal.

**"I am not discouraged because every wrong attempt discarded is another step forward."**
**—Thomas Edison**

Whenever you have prospect / customer complains about something to you, thank them for the complaint. Tell them that they have just improved your business because they brought this issue to your attention. The complaint will then go away.

## WHAT MAKES AN OPTIMUM LEADER?

### Tip # 4

To survive in the 21st century, we're going to need a new generation of leaders not managers.

Some crucial differences of a leader and a manager:

- The manager administers; the leader innovates.

- The manager is a copy; the leader is an original.

- The manager maintains; the leader develops.

- The manager relies on control; the leader inspires trust.

- The manager has a short-range view; the leader has a long-range perspective.

- The manager asks how and when; the leader asks what and why.

- The manager has their eye on the bottom line; the leader has their eye on the horizon.

- The manager accepts the status quo; the leader challenges it.

- The manager does things right; the leader does the right thing.

Leaders come in every size, shape and disposition.

Research from Warren Bennis as he talked with leaders, they shared at least one characteristic: a concern with a guiding purpose, a overarching vision.

They were more than goal-directed. They had a clear idea of what they want to do and the strength to persist in the face of setbacks, even failures. They know where they are going and why.

Leaders must be developed and nurtured.

## THINGS A LEADER CREATES

## Tip # 5

Warren Benis notes that lots of people spend their lives climbing a ladder and then they get to the top of the wrong wall.

Leading is about what and why.

Leadership is about trust—about people.

1. A leader creates a compelling vision.

If you want to lead people, first, get them to buy into a shared vision and then translate that vision into action. Leaders take people to a new place.

Leaders inspire and empower people; they pull rather than push.

2. A leader creates a climate of trust.

Remember: A lot of trust comes not from a particular technique, but from the character of the leader.

**To create trust, you need:**

a. Competence Followers have to have some trust in the leader's capacity to do the job.

b. Congruity The leader is a person of integrity. What you say is congruent with what you do, and that's congruent with what you feel, and that's congruent with what your vision is.

People would much rather follow individuals they can count on, even when they disagree with their viewpoint than people they agree with but who shift positions frequently.

c. Constancy People want a sense that their leader is on their side, that he or she will be constant.

These qualities a leader must embody to create and sustain trust.

3. A leader creates success.

—often from failure Successful leaders perceive and handle failure differently.

Leaders embrace error. They see failure as a mistake, a false start, or misdirection.

The thing about failure is that it demands explanation. The people who don't succeed are the people who look at failure and don't learn from it.

They blame somebody else not themselves.

Successful leaders learned to embrace error and learn from it. They keep the message moving, they make it clear to those they lead that there is no failure, only mistakes that give us feedback and tell us what to do next.

4.   A leader creates a healthy empowering environment.

Effective leadership empowers the workforce. They have a sense of human bond, a sense of community, a sense of meaning in their work. A feeling of significance is so important.

Good leaders make people feel that they're at the very heart of things, not at the periphery. Everyone feels that he or she makes a difference to the success of the organization.

Leadership gives the workforce a sense of meaning, of significance, of competence, of community, of commitment rather than compliance. It also gives the workforce a sense of fun.

5.   A leader creates flat, flexible, adaptive organizations.

Bureaucracies don't create leaders; they create managers.

Organizations that operate on the model of bureaucracy—based on the words control, order and predict—are not going to cut it.

Almost half (47%) of the organizations that were Fortune 500 companies between 1979 and 1989 are no longer there because they weren't adaptive enough.

We need more leadership and less bureaucracy. It's either change or die.

# THREE WAYS TO KILL CREATIVE LEADERSHIP

## Tip # 6

You can kill and bury creative leadership in the following ways"

1.   Emphasize managing instead of pioneering.

Many US companies are very well managed, but poorly led. Routine work smothers creativity and change. We immerse ourselves in routine and avoid the tough questions.

2.   Insist on harmony and pseudo-agreement.

The cohesiveness of most organizations depends on a commonly held set of values. Anyone who does not share the common culture is an outsider.

But unanimity leads to stagnation. The individual who sees things differently is the company's vital link to change and adaptation. Every leader needs at least one fool to challenge what is sacred.

3.   Reward non-achievers.

Remember those who do the work deserve the pay.

Lead by example, judge by results.

Everyone needs ambition, expertise and integrity.

# THREE ABILITIES TO LOOK FOR:

## Tip # 7

To have breakthrough leadership, churches, companies need these three qualities:

1. Ability to articulate a vision.

Leaders must create a compelling vision that takes people to a new place and then translate that vision into reality.

2. Ability to embrace error.

Failure, error and mistakes all require explanation. The ability to embrace error is an important component in creating an atmosphere in which risk taking is encouraged. Sydney Pollard, a successful film director, tells his people, the only mistake is to do nothing.

3. Ability to encourage reflective back talk.

Real leaders know the importance of having someone around who will tell the truth.

Warren Bennis, in his research on chief executives found that their spouse was a person they could totally trust. The back talk from the spouse, the trusted one is reflective because it allows the leader to learn, to find out more about himself or herself.

## THREE QUESTIONS TO ASK:

### Tip # 8

A leader's effectiveness can be gauged by asking these three questions:

1. Do people feel significant?

When a leader is truly leading, people feel that what they do has meaning.

2. Is the work felt to be exciting?

Leaders will pull not push people toward a goal. They do so by making the work stimulating, challenging, and fun. This pull style of influence attracts and energizes people, motivating them to achieve by identification.

3. Does the leader embody the organization's ethics and values?

Sending mix messages to the organization on ethical issues, more than anything else, is one of the most destructive things a leader can do.

It has been said, "We must be the change we wish to see in the world."

The status quo will not help us much ahead. That's a guarantee.

## THE BENEFITS OF GOOD LEADERSHIP ARE:

## Tip # 9

- The team works as a team not just as a group of individuals. It works to achieve a common objective.

- The team is able to understand its objectives and how these fit in with overall organizational objectives.

- Team members support each other.

- The team is prepared to put in extra effort when required.

- The team aims for excellence, not just "doing the job".

- Everyone knows what the team has to do, and their role in doing it.

- Team members are motivated to do what needs to be done.

# THE COST OF BAD LEADERSHIP IS:

## Tip # 10

- The group is unclear on what it has to do.

- The group is not motivated.

- The individuals are not working as a team and will not perform as well as a real team would.

- The group will probably only do enough to get the job done and won't be able to sustain a workload under pressure.

- The group members will leave more often, as they will not want to stay in such an environment.

- Individuals will not develop the necessary skills, and the group will be unable to deal with new situations.

## EMPOWERMENT: THE EFFECT OF LEADERSHIP

## Tip # 11

Leadership gives pace and energy to the work and empowers the organization.

Empowerment is evident in:

1. People feel significant.

Everyone feels that he or she makes a difference to the success of the organization.

2. Learning and competence matters.

Leaders value learning.

3.  People are part of a community.

Where there is leadership, there is a team, a family, a unity.

4.  Work is exciting.

Work is stimulating, challenging and fun.

# CHAPTER
## X

*Final laws of Optimum Leadership*

# FINELY THE LAW OF POSITIVE SELF-AFFIRMATIONS

1.  God loves me more than I can ever imagine and I am never beyond the reach of this great Love.

*"I'm absolutely convinced that nothing—nothing living or dead, angelic or demonic, today or tomorrow, high or low, thinkable or unthinkable—absolutely nothing can get between us and God's love because of the way that Jesus our Master has embraced us."—(Romans 8:39 The Bible)*

2.  No matter what my sin, God forgives me if I repent, confess and turn my life over to Him.

*"If we claim that we're free of sin, we're only fooling ourselves. A claim like that is errant nonsense. On the other hand, if we admit our sins—make a clean breast of them—he won't let us down; he'll be true to himself. He'll forgive our sins and purge us of all wrongdoing. If we claim that we've never sinned, we out-and-out contradict God—make a liar out of him. A claim like that only shows off our ignorance of God."—(1 John 1:9 The Bible)*

3.  There is nothing I can do that will cause God to turn away from me.

*"Don't be obsessed with getting more material things. Be relaxed with what you have. Since God assured us, "I'll never let you down, never walk off and leave you," we can boldly quote,*

> *God is there, ready to help;*
> *I'm fearless no matter what.*
> *Who or what can get to me?"—(Hebrews 13:5 The Bible)*

4.  Whatever I attempt to do, if it is God's will for me, He will give me the strength and wisdom I need to accomplish it.

*"Whatever I have, wherever I am, I can make it through anything in the One who makes me who I am."—(Philippians 4:13 The Bible)*

5.  If I seem to fail because circumstances are against me, God will always give me another opportunity if I return to the starting point.

*"Stalwart walks in step with GOD; his path blazed by GOD, he's happy. If he stumbles, he's not down for long; GOD has a grip on his hand."—(Psalms 37:24 The Bible)*

6.  God never wants to give up.

*All your life, no one will be able to hold out against you. In the same way I was with Moses, I'll be with you. I won't give up on you; I won't leave you . . . . Give it everything you have, heart and soul. Make sure you carry out The Revelation that Moses commanded you, every bit of it. Don't get off track, either left or right, so as to make sure you get to where you're going; then you'll succeed . . . Haven't I commanded you? Strength! Courage! Don't be timid; don't get discouraged. GOD, your God, is with you every step you take."—(Joshua 1:5,7,9 The Bible)NKJV*

**"In order to succeed, you must know what you are doing, and believe in what you are doing."—Will Rogers**

Character? Think of it as the product of core values and moral courage, in other words it is a person who chooses Everyday Optimum Leadership as a way of life.

Someone once said, "Character in not one more thing to learn to put on your plate, **IT IS YOUR PLATE.**"

### SECRETS to HAPPINESS

1.  Live below your means.
2.  Return everything you borrow.
3.  Donate blood.
4.  Stop blaming other people.
5.  Admit it when you make a mistake.
6.  Everyday do something nice and try not to get caught.

7. Listen more. Talk less.
8. Everyday take a 30 minute walk in your neighborhood.
9. Strive for excellence—not perfection.
10. Skip 2 meals a week and give the money to the needy.
11. Be on time.
12. Don't make excuses.
13. Don't argue.
14. Get organized.
15. Be kind to kind people.
16. Be even kinder to unkind people.
17. Let someone cut ahead of you in line.
18. Take time to be alone.
19. Reread a favorite book.
20. Cultivate good manners.
21. Be humble.
22. Understand and accept that life isn't always fair.
23. Know when to say something.
24. Know when to keep your mouth shut.
25. Don't criticize anyone for 24 hours.
26. Learn from the past, plan for the future and live in the present.
27. Don't sweat the small stuff.
28. It's all small stuff.

## The Secret of Happiness

### Psalm 1

Blessed *is* the man Who walks not in the counsel of the ungodly, Nor stands in the path of sinners, Nor sits in the seat of the scornful But his delight *is* in the law of the LORD, And in His law he meditates day and night. He shall be like a tree Planted by the rivers of water, That brings forth its fruit in its season, Whose leaf also shall not wither; And whatever he does shall prosper. The ungodly *are* not so, But are like the chaff which the wind drives away. Therefore the ungodly shall not stand in the judgment, Nor sinners in the congregation of the righteous. For the LORD knows the way of the righteous, But the way of the ungodly shall perish.

## 1.  Psalm 1

**To be blessed is to enjoy divine grace and favor, which alone brings true happiness.** Happiness is the goal of every soul on earth. Sad to say, more often than not, people look for happiness in the wrong places. Not surprisingly therefore, comparatively few find true happiness.

- Many believe that the **more money** they can lay their hands on the happier they will be: so they exhaust themselves making money. But rich people are not the happiest folk on earth.
- Others believe that **fame** will bring happiness; so they put forth giant efforts to become famous. But famous people are by no means the happiest people either.
- Still others believe that **beauty** will bring happiness; so they spend fortunes on looking beautiful. But beautiful people are not happier than ugly people.
- Others think **possessions, position, authority, power** or **knowledge** will bring happiness. But they too fail to obtain true happiness.

We see this all around—in every country—people possessing all these desirable things and still being unhappy: or rather they are no happier than those without these things. And so we ask:

**'Where and how can one find happiness? What does one have to do or not do to obtain this illusive thing called happiness?**

**Psalm 1** gives us the answer to these vital questions.

## 2.  Where Happiness is not found

To begin with this psalm lists **three places** where happiness is **not** found. The man (or woman) who finds true happiness will certainly **not** do these three things:

**Verse 1**

- **He will not walk in the counsel of the ungodly.** In other words in moral matters he will not follow the advice of those who knowingly and blatantly disobey the Almighty's commandments.
- **He will not stand in the way of sinners.** In other words, he will not just refuse to walk in the counsel of sinners; but will not make friends with them.
- **He will not sit in the seat of the scornful.** In other words he will never take part in mocking sacred things.

Note the progression: first **walking**, then **standing**, and finally **sitting** with evil associates and their ways. True happiness is never found in such company or behavior. The Bible says:

Isaiah 57:20 *But the wicked are like the troubled sea, when it cannot rest, whose waters cast up mire and dirt. 21: There is no peace, says God, to the wicked.*

**3. Where then is Happiness Found?**

The psalm then goes on to tell us where true happiness (blessing) is found. The blessed man will:

**Verse 2**

- **Delight in the law of the Almighty.** This implies that the law of the Almighty is a gateway to true happiness. The happy man will search it out and enter in. He will take **delight** in studying Jehovah's commandments, and in obeying them as best he can. This is the pathway to true happiness. This is the first spiritual clue to finding true happiness. Remember it!
- **The happy (blessed) man or woman will meditate on Yahweh's law day and night.** In other words he/she will ponder and think about the deep truths hidden in the Almighty's

commandments: truths which can only be understood with **spiritual assistance** from on high. The happy person will think about these things and continually request **understanding** and **wisdom** from God Himself. The Apostle James writes:

James 1:5 *If any of you lack wisdom, let him ask of God, that gives to all men liberally, and upbraideth not; and it shall be given him.*

The Apostle Paul writes:

Philippians 4:8 *Finally, brethren, whatsoever things are true, whatsoever things are honest, whatsoever things are just, whatsoever things are pure, whatsoever things are lovely, whatsoever things are of good report; if there be any virtue, and if there be any praise, **think on these things**.*

## 3. The Results

The results of this simple yet profound spiritual formula—of **meditating on Yahweh's law and putting it into practice**—will produce blessing and happiness on an ever-increasing scale. Note that these blessings produce **true happiness**. They are not dependent on material wealth, possessions, power or fame, but on **faithful obedience** to God. The blessed (happy) man or woman, as the Psalmist goes on to say will:

### Verse 3

- **Have an everlasting source of spiritual refreshment.** He/she will be like an evergreen, river-side tree; which produces a constant supply of delicious fruit.
- **Prosper in everything he/she does.** In other words, whatever he attempts will meet with success. It will produce lasting and worthwhile results.

## WHAT PEOPLE WANT FROM THEIR LEADERS:

Four Characteristics that Standout:

### 1. Purpose, Direction and Meaning.

A strong determination to achieve a goal.

### 2. Trust.

The trust factor is the social glue that keeps any act together.

To trust other people, to have confidence in them, we need to see evidence of competence. We expect our leaders to be competent.

Another aspect of trust is openness. Listening builds trust. Listening doesn't mean agreeing, but it does mean understanding another.

### 3. A sense of we-can-do-it optimism.

Leaders need to perceive that they can really change the world.

### 4. Action and results.

A quality common to leaders is the capacity to convert purpose and vision into action.

**Wayne Gretsky said, "You miss 100 percent of the shots you don't take."**

## SUGGESTIONS for a BRIGHTER FUTURE

1. Realize that life isn't always fair. Accept what you must and change what you can.

2. Think before you act. A moment of carelessness or anger can cause months of anguish and regret.

3. Look for the beauty in life, in people and in yourself.

4. Appreciate what you have: the people, the opportunities and the material possessions.

5. Make the effort to have fun: it's a great way to bond with others, and it makes some of the best memories.

6. Set-aside some time for yourself. Do something you enjoy without feeling even a little guilty.

7. Accept others without judgment. Everyone is unique and it's okay to be different.

8. Forgive. Bitterness and resentment hurt you more than the person you direct them at.

9. Learn. Open your mind to new ideas and activities and don't be afraid to try.

## LIFE-CHANGING DECLARATIONS

1. I completely forgive myself.

2. I completely love myself.

3. I control my own life.

4. Everyday I will learn something new.

5. I let myself be loved by others.

6. I bring balance into my life daily.

7. I go easy on myself.

8. I create my own life.

9. I find work that satisfies me and rewards me.

10. I live in the present.

11. Bringing new experiences into my life is something I try to do monthly.

12. I keep moving forward.

13. I will live by the golden rule.

14. I can change only myself.

15. Self-leadership is my goal.

16. Continually I rearrange my thoughts.

17. I am a sharing and caring person.

18. I stand strong.

19. I can and will always smile.

20. I like to have fun.

21. Every human being has worth.

22. Love and laughter control my life.

23. My mind and heart guide my decisions.

24. I discipline myself daily.

## POSITIVE SELF-AFFIRMATIONS

1.  God loves me more than I can ever imagine and I am never beyond the reach of this great love. (Rom. 8:39)
2.  No matter what my sin, God forgives me if I repent, confess and return to Him. (1John 1:9 & Ps 103:10-12)
3.  There is nothing I can do that will cause God to turn away from me. (Heb 13:5)
4.  Whatever I attempt to do, if it is God's will for me, He will give me the strength and wisdom I need to accomplish it. (Phil 4:13)
5.  If I seem to fail because circumstances are against me, God will always give me another opportunity if I return to the starting point. (Ps 37:24)
6.  God never wants to give up. (Josh 1:5,7,9)

## THINGS to REMEMBER

1.  Your presence is a present to the world.

2.  You are unique and one of a kind.

3.  Your life can be what you want it to be with God leading.

4.  Count your blessings, not your troubles.

5.  You will make it through whatever comes along.

6.  If you ask, God will place within you the answers.

7.  Understand, have courage, be strong.

8.  Do not put limits on yourself.

9.  Your dreams are waiting to be realized.

10. Nothing wastes more energy than worrying.

11. The longer one carries a problem, the heavier it gets.

12. Do not take things too seriously.

13. Live a life of serenity not a life of regrets.

14. Remember that a little love goes a long way.

15. Remember that friendship is a wise investment.

16. Realize that it is never too late.

## HOW to GET OUT of the RUT and STAY OUT of IT

1.  Stop listening to negative influences. Misery loves company. Get around someone who is doing well and emulate the positive aspects of their habits and attitudes.

2.  Set some new goals. Goals create focus and can be daily motivators when they are INSPIRING and STRETCHING you. They help put distractions aside and keep you going through setbacks.

3.  Focus on what you have, not on what you don't. Count your blessings (which are many, if not sure ask me).

4.  Focus on what you can control. You can control your attitude, your disciplines, your work ethic, your time, and your associations. You can't control the attitudes of others.

5.  Do something to create personal momentum. Develop or refine a skill. Call a good positive friend and go for coffee or tea. Develop new eating habits. Read something positive and uplifting every morning and every evening.

6. Take time to reflect and make adjustments. I don't mean to withdraw!!! Assess your direction, determine what you've done right and wrong and make adjustments.

7. Do something for another person. Nothing breaks our self-centered grip like serving another. Give yourself away, believing that giving starts the receiving process.

## DECLARATION of SELF-ESTEEM

I am ME. I am made in the image of God, just a little lower than the angels. I am unique. In all the world there is no one exactly like me. The Bible says that I am awesome and fearfully made. Everything about me was designed for His work because God said so. My body. My mind, My spirit, My dreams, My talents, My feelings (positive and negative). My words. All my thoughts and actions can make a unique contribution to life.

I can accept myself because God accepts me. I can love myself because God loves me. I know I matter because God in the form of Jesus Christ gave me the chance to live abundantly and eternally. I do not have to be perfect to be loved because God loved me while I was imperfect, while I was a lost sinner.

This means my value is not dependent on my position in life but on what the Bible tells me. Even when I have "rough edges" in my life and when I make mistakes, even big ones. I can fail. I can stumble. God still says, "I love you!" I don't have to have everything in the right order, or have everything cleaned up for God to accept me. I just ask Him into my life, ask Him to forgive me of my sins and mean it in my heart. Then He will make me a new person in Christ. His word tells me that he will do just that.

By knowing that, I can live with myself. And I have hope that I can take all that I am and all that I have to God (the good and the bad) and He will keep on improving me. I can be totally honest. I have something to look forward to. With His help and guidance I will be even more effective in living, loving, and serving others than I have been. Tomorrow will be better than today. I turn my life over to Him.

I am not afraid to keep at the lifelong task of learning, growing, and becoming the best I can be with God's word and the Holy Spirit as my teacher. God gives me His grace and along with that and all of my faculties to work at the task of pressing forward I am His.

So I accept the fact that God loves me and that He can use me in this life. I have eternal value and it is okay to be ME because I am His and He is mine.

Signed_____ Date_____

# Afterword

Well, if you have read though the book, hopefully taken the "Leadership Instruments," I pray you will allow the Lord to speak to your heart about Servant Leadership and being what I called "Other Centered Focused." The take-ways from this book are not that profound or lofty but remain down to earth and practical for the person who wants to follow the greatest servant leader in history, Jesus Christ. Because all of the precepts, concepts and principles used in this work came directly from God's word. Oh, they may have sometimes been served up using business concepts and language but at the core of every one of them is the solid truth only found in God's word.

In today's world the person working in a business or in a church finds themselves in a culture devoid of even the basic elements we talked about in this book. It is becoming harder and harder for anybody to "do the right thing," but it must be done. Optimum Leaders must take a stand for right living, right leading and right thinking.

As I stated at the beginning of the book, it was not my intention to write another boring book on leadership, but to present many of what I called HANDS ON and SNAP SHOOT bits to move the reader from one point to the next not necessarily connecting the two together but having each chapter and sometimes each page develop a brand new idea, tidbit or nugget to think about.

In Romans 12:1-3 Paul tell us . . ."*Therefore, I urge you brother, in view of God's mercy, to offer your bodies as living sacrifices, holy and pleasing to God—this is your spiritual act of worship. Do not conform any longer to the pattern of this world, but be transformed by the renewing of your mind. Then you will be able to test and approve what God's will is—His good, pleasing, and perfect will." (NIV)*

In regard to being an Everyday Optimum Leader please look at a few points with me.

Point #1) First Paul addresses our physical bodies and tells us to offer them as living sacrifices. But for anyone to do this it first starts on the inside, deep in the inner resting place of our will, and that is where operating with Everyday Optimum Leadership comes in. Remember I said, "It all starts on the inside." In order for your body or mine to be placed on the alter YOU or I have to decide to place it there and then the real hard part comes, having the inner strength <u>to keep it there</u>. And that is what Paul addresses next.

Point #2) Paul states that we must not be conformed to this world, but be TRANSFORMED by the renewing of our minds. BINGO . . . this is the heart of this book. The purpose of this writing was to; by the power of the Holy Spirit and the truth of God's word give the reader some practical tools to help with the transformation process. To start work on the inside and in doing to create deep down in the heart, the birth of a new YOU an Everyday Optimum Leader.

Live each and every day in the knowledge, grace, and mercy of God's word and the power of the Holy Spirit. Be the **Everyday Optimum Leader** you can be.

## REMEMBER

*"Future intentions are determined by present action."*

Rex Wolins

# About the Author

Mr. Wolins is a pastor, gifted speaker and lecturer, a strong communicator and cultivator of personal skills for managers and leaders in the church and in the marketplace. The Lord has used him in ministry and in the business arena for over 30 years. His background includes:

- Consultant for The Billy Graham Evangelistic Association Los Angeles California
- Consultant for Teen Challenge Missoula Montana "Taking a Stand for God, Family & Country," with key note speaker Governor Sarah Palin
- On staff as General Crusade Director for the Somebody Loves You Crusades with Pastor Raul Ries
- Senior Pastor Christian Church of the Hills in Agoura California
- Supervising Chaplain for the Los Angeles Sheriff's Department
- Level one Reserve Patrol Deputy for the Los Angeles Sheriff's Department

Experienced in capital fund raising for building expansion projects in the for-profit and non-profit sector he has worked with large leadership teams of people to facilitate growth in churches and companies across the United States and in other countries including New Zealand, Bogotá Colombia, Peru, Chile, North Africa and China. He has lead executive and associate leadership training seminars for many large companies like Risco insurance Inc., Citizens Bank Corporate office and E.O. International Inc. among others.

Mr. Wolins is the Director of Optimum Leadership Consulting, a 501 (c) 3 non-profit company located in Walnut California. www. optimumleadership.vpweb.com

He holds a Bachelor of Science in Business Management from The University of Phoenix, A Master of Arts Degree from Hope International University and a second Master of Organizational Leadership Degree from Biola University.

He lives in Walnut California with his wife Shi Mei. They have a daughter Nancy Roettger, she and her husband live in Riverside California.

# PERSONAL NOTES

# PERSONAL NOTES

# PERSONAL NOTES

# Bibliography

Drucker, Peter, F. (1989) <u>The New Realities: In Government and Politics</u>: in Economics and Business: in Society and World View New York: Harper & Row Publishing.

Drucker, Peter, F (1985) <u>The Effective Executive</u>, p. 130

Frankl, E. Viktor (1959) <u>Man's Search for Meaning</u> A Touchstone Book Published by Siimon & Schuster New York, London

Hill, Alexander (1997) <u>Just Business</u> Inter Varsity Press Downers Grove Ill

Hill, W. L. Charles (1997) <u>International Business—Competing in the Global Marketplace</u> Irwin / McGraw—Hill Publishing

James, Miller (1995) <u>The Empowered Leader</u>

Jardins, R. Joseph (1997) <u>Environmental Ethics</u> Wadsworth Publishing Company

Kouzes, M. James & Posner Z. Barry <u>The Leadership Challenge</u> (1995) Jossey-Bass A Wiley Company San Francisco CA

Kouzes and Posner, (1993) <u>The Leadership Challenge</u>, pp. 16-17

Madsen, Ola Dr. (2008) <u>Everyday Leadership</u> A guide for today's leader

Northouse, G. Peter (2001) <u>Leadership Theory and Practice</u> Sage Publication, Inc. Thousand Oaks Ca

Payne, T. (May 11,1993) Passage—Getting from Here to There During Change Supervision 54, p.11.

Peterson H. Eugene, (1993) The Message Translation NavPress Publishing Group Colorado Springs, CO.

Ries A. Raul, (1999) Five Deadly Vices pp. 26-30 Logos Media Group

Diamond Bar CA

Reflections on Leadership, *"Introduction: Servant-Leadership and The Greenleaf Legacy"* (p. 4-7) by Larry Spears

Robert K. Greenleaf, (1997) Leadership, pp. 13-14

Robbins, Stephen P. (2003) Organizational Behavior Prentice Hall Publishing Upper Saddle River, New Jersey. P. 20.

Smedley, F. Ronald (2002) Leadership & group behavior Class notes 5th edition, MOL 610 Biola University La Mirada CA.

Staw, B. M. & Cummings, L. L. (1996) Research in Organizational Behavior Volume. 18 Greenwich, CT: JAI Press pp. 1-3.

The American Heritage® Dictionary of English Language, Fourth Edition

Scripture. (1973, 1978, 1984) The Holy Bible International Bible Society Zondervan

Wofford, J.C. (1982) Organizational Behavior: Foundation for Organizational Effectiveness Boston, MA: Kent Publishing Company. Pp. 397-398.

WordNet ® 1.6 © (1997 Princeton University